Augustus Pugin, Richard Phené Spiers

Specimens of the Architecture of Normandy

From the 16th to the 17th century. Engraved by John and Henry Le Keux

Augustus Pugin, Richard Phené Spiers

Specimens of the Architecture of Normandy
From the 16th to the 17th century. Engraved by John and Henry Le Keux

ISBN/EAN: 9783337328306

Printed in Europe, USA, Canada, Australia, Japan

Cover: Foto ©ninafisch / pixelio.de

More available books at **www.hansebooks.com**

SPECIMENS

OF THE

ARCHITECTURE OF NORMANDY,

FROM THE XIth TO THE XVIth CENTURY.

MEASURED AND DRAWN

By AUGUSTUS PUGIN, Architect;

ENGRAVED BY JOHN AND HENRY LE KEUX.

WITH HISTORICAL AND DESCRIPTIVE NOTICES BY JOHN BRITTON, F.S.A.

NEW EDITION, EDITED BY

RICHARD PHENÉ SPIERS, A.R.I.B.A.,

MASTER OF THE ARCHITECTURAL SCHOOL OF THE ROYAL ACADEMY; TRAVELLING STUDENT, ETC.

LONDON:
BLACKIE & SON, PATERNOSTER BUILDINGS, E.C.;
GLASGOW AND EDINBURGH.
1874.

PREFACE.

Though a number of years have elapsed since the first publication of Pugin and Le Keux' Architectural Antiquities of Normandy, it is still regarded as the chief standard Work on the architecture of that country; and it would be difficult to select better examples for publication than those which were chosen by Pugin, notwithstanding our far greater knowledge of the country and its buildings at the present day. It would scarcely be too much to assert that no work has appeared since, which by the beauty of its engravings and the accuracy of the measured drawings they represent, has a greater claim to the careful study of every architect, draughtsman, or archæologist, who seeks to realize for himself the development of French architecture in Normandy during five and a half centuries.

In fact, when we consider the immense progress which has taken place during the last forty years in the true knowledge of medieval architecture, and how, step by step, the vague theories of its rise and development have been displaced by sound scientific knowledge, we are astounded that drawings, made so long ago, should not only show a perfect mastery of rule and compass, but display the most intimate acquaintance with all the artistic and scientific problems of the buildings represented. In these drawings the formation of the ribs and webs of vaulting, their true curvatures, and the constructive lines of every part of the buildings, are indicated with a truth that few draughtsmen of the present day could hope to rival; whilst the character and vigour of the foliage, and other carved ornament, especially that of the Flamboyant period, has been rendered in a manner that has never been equalled in any more recent publication.

Photography and the development of lithographic drawing have now unfortunately in this country almost superseded the more tedious and expensive process of line engraving; but, whether for beauty and perfection of drawing, or for accuracy in the lines, the latter must ever be pre-eminent. The great reputation of the Le Keuxs as architectural engravers, is fully sustained by the admirable plates in this work on the architecture of Normandy.

To the architectural student the work is of twofold interest.

1st. It shows the exact nature of the kind of drawing it is most useful to make when engaged in measuring or delineating ancient work.

2d. The drawings give a succinct yet complete history of the successive phases of the Norman style, of the development of Pointed Architecture, and of its ultimate decadence in that province of France, which, to British architects and archæologists, is by far the most interesting. Thus, in the illustrations of the "Abbaye aux Hommes," and "Abbaye aux Dames," and the Church of St. Nicholas, at Caen—the Churches of Thaon near Caen, of St. Loup near Bayeux, and portions of Bayeux Cathedral—the student will find the most perfect series of the successive phases of the Norman style; in the choirs of the "Abbaye aux Hommes," Caen, and of Bayeux Cathedral—and in the tower of St. Peter's at Caen—that variety of thirteenth-century architecture which prevailed in Normandy, and which, while it presents so many differences in detail and execution from the architecture of the Isle of France, assimilates so much to our own.

In the Plates of St. Ouen, Rouen, are presented a series of drawings of the most complete and typical specimen of fourteenth-century French Gothic; whilst in those of the Palais de Justice, the Fountains, the Hôtel Bourgtheroulde, the "Abbaye St. Amand," the staircases and other features of Notre Dame, and the Church of St. Maclou, all at Rouen—the doorway of St. Michael, Vaucelles, in Caen—and the Church at Caudebec—the application of the French Flamboyant architecture of the fifteenth century, to both secular and ecclesiastical buildings, is delineated with an accuracy and vigour to be fully appreciated only by those who have attempted to transfer to paper its intricate and delicate forms.

In the choice of examples the selections for illustration are so made and arranged that the student is led step by step through that development of style which, starting with the simple, bold architecture of the early Norman period, and passing through all those stages of progress in which the pointed arch forms so essential a feature, arrives at the most exquisite and elaborate forms of Flamboyant work, thence leading almost imperceptibly into the early French Renaissance.

The emendations and additions made in this edition are as follows: The plates have undergone a careful revision, and it will be found that the impressions now furnished may compare with those in the first edition without disadvantage. With exception of two plates hitherto tinted by hand, and which, from their crudeness of colour, were apt to deceive rather than guide the student, the whole series, extending to seventy-eight plates, is published in its integrity. A plan of the "Abbaye aux Dames," Caen, measured and drawn by the Editor expressly for this edition, forms an additional plate. With exception of a small woodcut in a work by M. Ruprich Robert, no plan of this interesting building has been published hitherto.

In the revision of the text the Editor has deemed it expedient to strike out all those parts which subsequent investigations have shown to be inexact and fallacious. The greater portion of the text is re-arranged, and a more complete and satisfactory description of every building illustrated is given, the dates being corrected where necessary. An account is also added of the development of Gothic vaulting, tracing its history by means of the illustrated examples. To a considerable extent the additional information is given in the form of extracts from the works of

viii   PREFACE TO THE FIRST EDITION.

recent authors whose writings are considered authoritative. All the additions, whether in the text or notes, are distinguished by being inclosed in square brackets [   ]. With a view to this revision, the Editor has visited the greater number of the buildings illustrated, and has consulted all the books published on the subject, so far as he is aware of their existence, and of these last he appends a list for the benefit of such of his readers as may desire to pursue this study farther.

LONDON, *April*, 1874.   R. PHENÉ SPIERS.

PREFACE TO THE FIRST EDITION,

OMITTING SOME PORTIONS THAT HAVE CEASED TO BE OF INTEREST.

THE present work originated with the Artists whose names appear in the title-page; and who, from predilection for architectural antiquities, and from some experience in the execution of works illustrative of the ancient buildings in England, persuaded themselves that a series of Engravings, which should define and clearly exemplify the Christian Architecture of Normandy, would be at once useful and popular. Influenced by corresponding feelings and conviction, the writer of this Preface was induced to co-operate with his friends, and enter warmly and zealously into the plan. He wrote a prospectus, assisted in arranging and digesting the work, and advised with Mr. Pugin previous to his visits to Normandy. It was also his intention, when he first engaged in the work, to see and examine all the buildings delineated, and to write the accounts of them after careful examination.[1] This intention was

[1] This has always been his practice with the *Architectural and Cathedral Antiquities*, in which works he has devoted much time to local investigations, and many hundreds of pounds in collecting materials and in travelling expenses.

frustrated by illness, at the very time when he had prepared for a journey into Normandy. Thus disappointed, he wrote down particular instructions, and sent them, with letters of inquiry, to distinguished antiquaries in the province. Waiting for, and expecting answers,—anxious to render the history and description of each building, and of every variety of architecture, original, accurate, and discriminating, he has delayed the publication, and even now has been impelled to hasten it through the press, without obtaining the answers and information he sought for, and consequently without satisfying himself in many parts of its execution.

It may be necessary to explain the reason of affixing the word *Editor* to the name of the writer of this Preface,—a thing so unusual to him,—for there are still many persons, even in England, who do not clearly discriminate the distinction between that and the word *Author*. According to the most correct interpretation, the latter applies strictly and exclusively to the writer of a book or literary essay; and Editor means the person who superintends, directs, and occasionally writes a part or parts of a miscellaneous publication, such as a newspaper, magazine, review, &c. The Author, as Gibbon, Hume, Sir Walter Scott, &c., is the writer, the sole composer, of a book, to which his name is attached: whilst the Editor, as Campbell, Lockhart, Barnes, &c., is the director, and partly the writer, of a periodical work, such as the *New Monthly Magazine*, the *Quarterly Review*, *The Times:* by the same rule, the writer of this Preface is Editor of the volume, and also author of its principal contents. He likewise edited two former volumes of a corresponding class, entitled *"Specimens of Gothic Architecture;"* but in that instance did not insert his name in the title-page; nor was he at all desirous of announcing it, or taking the responsibility of the present publication. Averse as he always has been to anonymous writings, he deemed it most honourable to avow his name on this occasion, and be at once amenable for defects as he is entitled to his fair portion of credit. He deems it

PREFACE TO THE FIRST EDITION.

merely justice to himself to make this explanation, which will also account for the origin and completion of the volume; and this he hopes will give the student in ancient architecture more satisfaction than it has afforded to himself. His views and wishes at the commencement were to investigate the history, and definitely characterize the ancient architecture of Normandy,—to ascertain and point out what is really indigenous and what is exotic,—to show when and by whom its various changes of style were effected, and how these were progressively improved,—to seek diligently and scrupulously to ascertain the origin of the pointed style, and to compare and contrast the correspondencies and varieties of the architecture of Normandy with the contemporary architecture of England. These points he considered to be desiderata in English literature, and these he had marked out to himself as objects for inquiry and for accomplishment. Thwarted in his wishes and intentions, he looks forward with anxiety to THE SOCIETY OF ANTIQUARIES OF NORMANDY for the accomplishment of this, or for something of the like nature; and from the Essays already published by that Society, and from the zeal and knowledge some of its enlightened members have evinced, he is persuaded that such a publication can be produced by them jointly, if not by any single member. To that Society the writer of this Preface tenders his best wishes and thanks, for the compliment they have paid him in making him an *Honorary Member.* To JOHN COLES, Esq., DAWSON TURNER, Esq., and Mr. S. TYMMS, he is also obliged for useful hints, and to the latter gentleman for some of the ensuing Essays.

J. BRITTON.

LONDON, *June* 20, 1828.

LIST OF THE ENGRAVINGS,

ARRANGED IN NEARLY A CHRONOLOGICAL SERIES, ACCORDING TO THE TESTIMONIES OF DIFFERENT AUTHORS.

PLATE		PAGE
	CAEN, near.—CHAPEL OF LA GRANDE MALADRERIE, *Frontispiece.*	31
I.	. . . WINDOW AND DETAILS.	
	—— CHURCH OF ST. STEPHEN.—*L'Abbaye aux Hommes,*	33
II.	. . . GROUND PLAN of the Abbey Church.	
III.	. . . Exterior Perspective View from the North-west.	
IV.	. . . INTERIOR, Perspective View.	
V.	. . . NAVE, Exterior Elevation, Transverse Section, and Plan of Compartment.	
VI.	. . . NAVE, Interior Elevation of two Compartments.	
VII.	. . . SACRISTY, Transverse Section, Plan, and Details.	
VIII.	. . . SACRISTY, Longitudinal Section.	
IX.	. . . CHOIR, Exterior and Interior, Elevation and Section of One Compartment.	
X. XI.	. . . APSE, Elevation, Section, and Plan of One Compartment.	
XII.	. . . DECORATIVE FEATURES, Details of.	
	—— CHURCH OF THE HOLY TRINITY.—*L'Abbaye aux Dames,* . .	44
XIII.	. . . ENTRANCE GATEWAY, Elevation, Section, and Plan.	
XIV.	. . . CRYPT beneath East End of the Choir, Plan, and Two Sections.	
XV.	. . . CAPITALS and BASES from the Crypt, Nave, and Transept.	
XVI.	. . . INTERIOR, Perspective View, looking East.	
XVI^a.	. . . GROUND PLAN of the Abbey Church.	
XVII.	. . . NAVE, Interior, Elevation of a Compartment, Section, and Details.	
	—— CHURCH OF ST. NICHOLAS, ...	51
XVIII.	. . . APSE, Transverse Section, Plan, and Details.	
XIX.	. . . APSE, Exterior Elevation and Longitudinal Section.	
	—— near.—THAON CHURCH, ...	53
XX.	. . . SOUTH ELEVATION, Plan and Details.	

LIST OF THE ENGRAVINGS.

PLATE		PAGE
	CAEN, near.—*Thaon Church,*	
XXI.	. . East and West Ends, Elevation and Details.	
XXII.	. . . Tower, Elevation, Section, and Plans.	
	BAYEUX, near.—Church of St. Loup, ...	55
XXIII.	Tower of the Church, Elevation, Plans, and Details.	
	BAYEUX, Cathedral of, ...	56
XXIV.	. . Ground Plan of the whole Building.	
XXV. XXVI.	. . . West Front, Elevation.	
XXVII.	. . . Interior, Perspective View from the West.	
XXVIII. XXIX.	. . . Nave, Elevation, Section, and Plans of a Compartment.	
XXX.	. . . Nave, Details of.	
XXXI. XXXII.	. . . Choir, Transverse Section of Half of the Choir, Two Aisles, and Crypt, with Plan.	
XXXIII. XXXIV.	. . . Choir, Elevation, Interior and Exterior of One Compartment, with Crypt.	
	CAEN.—Church of St. Peter, ...	63
XXXV. XXXVI.	. . . Tower and Spire, Elevation, Section, and Plans	
	—— Ducal Palace at, ...	64
XXXVII.	. . . Exterior and Interior, Elevation and Section, with Plan.	
	ROUEN.—Church of St. Ouen, ...	65
XXXVIII.	Ground Plan of the whole Building.	
XXXIX.	. . Interior, Perspective View, looking East.	
XL.	. . . Nave, Elevation and Transverse Section of One Compartment, with Aisle.	
XLI.	. . . Doorway on the South Side, Elevation and Section.	
XLII.	. . . Circular Window, West Front, Elevation.	
XLIII.	. . . Circular Window, West Front, one quarter shown large, with Sections.	
	—— Church of St. Vincent, ...	69
XLIV.	. . . West Porch, Plan and Section.	
XLV.	. . . West Porch, Elevation and Details.	

LIST OF THE ENGRAVINGS.

PLATE		PAGE
	ROUEN.—NUNNERY OF ST. CLAIR, ...	70
XLVI.	. . . GATEWAY, Elevation, Section, &c.	
	—— FOUNTAIN DE LA CROSSE, ...	70
XLVII.	. . . Elevation, Plan, and Details.	
	—— STONE CROSS AND CIRCULAR TURRET, ...	71
XLVIII. . . .	. . Elevation and Plan.	
	—— PALAIS DE JUSTICE, ...	71
XLIX.	. . . GROUND PLAN of the whole Buildings, Elevation of South Side, and Section of Salle des Procureurs.	
L.	. . . INTERIOR OF THE COURT, Perspective View.	
LI.	. . . SOUTH FRONT, Elevation of a Compartment, Section, and Details.	
LII.	. . . TURRET on the North Side, Elevation, Plan, and Details.	
LIII.	. . . WINDOW, North End of Hall, Elevation, Section, and Details.	
LIV.	. . . SALLE DES PROCUREURS, Staircase S.E. Angle, and Niche in do., Elevations and Sections.	
	—— HÔTEL DE BOURGTHEROULDE, ...	73
LV.	. . . FRONT ELEVATION, Section, &c.	
LVI.	. . . ELEVATION, Parts at large, and Details.	
	—— L'ABBAYE ST. AMAND, ...	75
LVII.	. . . BUILDING ON THE N. SIDE OF A COURT, Exterior Elevation, and Compartments at large.	
LVIII.	. . . CHIMNEY PIECE, Elevation, and Parts at Large.	
	—— CATHEDRAL OF NOTRE DAME, ...	77
LIX. .	. . . STAIRCASE in North Transept, Plan, Sections, and Details.	
LX.	STAIRCASE in North Transept, Elevation.	
LXI.	. . . DOORWAY on the North Side of the Cloisters, Elevation and Section.	
LXII. . . .	. . . GATEWAY to the Cour des Libraires, Elevation, Section, and Details.	
	CAEN.—CHURCH OF ST. MICHAEL, VAUCELLES, ...	79
LXIII. . . .	. . . NORTH PORCH, Elevation, Section, and Details.	
	CAUDEBEC.—CHURCH OF, ...	80
LXIV. . . .	. . . SACRISTY, Elevation, Section, and Details of Compartment.	
LXV.	. . . LADY CHAPEL, Plan, with Section and Details of Roof and Pendant.	

LIST OF THE ENGRAVINGS.

PLATE		PAGE
	ROUEN.—ARCHBISHOP'S PALACE, ...	82
LXVI. .	Two Turret Staircases, Elevations, Sections, and Plans.	
	—— Church of St. Maclou, ...	82
LXVII. .	Stone Staircase to Organ Loft, Elevation, Section, and Plans.	
	—— Palais de Justice and St. Andre Church, .	83
LXVIII.	Two Wooden Doors from.	
	CAEN.—Notre Dame, St. Peter's, and St. Stephen's, ...	83
LXIX.	Three Wooden Doors from.	
	DIEPPE.—Church of St. Jacques, ...	84
LXX.	Stone Screen in North Transept, Elevation and Section.	
	CAEN, near.—Château Fontaine-le-Henri, ...	85
LXXI. . . .	West Front, Perspective View.	
LXXII. .	Window, West Front, on Ground Floor of Tower.	
LXXIII.	Window, West Front, Upper Part of Tower.	
LXXIV.	BAYEUX AND ROUEN.—String-courses, from Notre Dame, Bayeux, and from St. Ouen, Palais de Justice, and St. Nicholas, Rouen, ...	87
LXXV. . . .	BAYEUX AND CAEN.—Parapets, from the Cathedral, Bayeux, and St. John's Church, Caen, ...	87
LXXVI.	CAEN AND ROUEN.—Decorative Details, from St. Ouen, Rouen, and Château Fontaine-le-Henri. . .	87
LXXVII. . .	ROUEN.—Examples showing the Leading of Stained Glass, from the Cathedral and St. Ouen, . .	88
LXXVIII. . .	—— Examples showing the Leading of Stained Glass, from the Cathedral and St. Ouen, ...	88

BOOKS RELATING TO NORMANDY

AND ITS

ARCHITECTURAL ANTIQUITIES.

The following is a List of the more important Books bearing directly on the subject. Those published prior to the issue of the first edition of this Work in 1827 were all consulted by Britton, and frequent reference is made to them; the others of subsequent dates have all been consulted for the present edition, and contain information which may be useful to those who desire to pursue the subject further. The titles of the Books are arranged chronologically in order of their publication, and those marked with an asterisk (*) are the more important from an architectural point of view:—

POMMERAYE (François).—Histoire de l'Abbaye de St. Ouen de Rouen,	fol. Rouen, 1662
Do. Histoire de l'Église Cathedral de Rouen (Plates),	4to, Rouen, 1686
DUCAREL (Andrew C.)—Anglo-Norman Antiquities (27 Copperplates),	fol. London, 1767
GUNN (William).—An Inquiry into the Origin and Influence of Gothic Architecture,	8vo, London, 1819
TURNER (Dawson).—Account of a Tour in Normandy, chiefly for the purpose of investigating its Architectural Antiquities; illustrated with numerous Engravings,	8vo, London, 1820
DE LA RUE (M. l'Abbé).—Essai Historique sur la Ville de Caen et ses Arrondissements,	8vo, Caen, 1820
LANGLOIS (Eustache H.)—Description Historique des Maisons de Rouen (40 Plates),	2 vols. 8vo, Rouen, 1821
STOTHARD (Mrs.)—Letters written during a Tour through Normandy and Brittany,	8vo, London, 1821
DIBDIN (Rev. T. F.)—Bibliographical, Antiquarian, and Picturesque Tour in France, with a vol. of illustrative Etchings by G. Lewis,	8vo, London, 1821
JOLIMONT (F. T. de).—Monumens les plus remarquables de la Ville de Rouen (30 Lithographs),	fol. Paris, 1822
*COTMAN (J. S.)—Architectural Antiquities of Normandy, represented in a series of 100 Etchings, with descriptive Notices by Dawson Turner,	fol. London, 1822
NODIER (Charles) and TAYLOR, I. J. S.—Voyages Pittoresques et Romantiques de l'Ancienne France (Normandie); many fine Lithographs,	fol. Paris, 1820-25
JOLIMONT (F. T. de).—Description historique et critique et Vues des Monuments religieux et civils les plus remarquables du Calvados (18 Lithographs),	4to, Paris, 1825

BOOKS RELATING TO NORMANDY, ETC.

LANGLOIS (Eustache H.)—Notice sur l'Incendie de la Cathedrale de Rouen en 1822, 8vo, Rouen, 1833
*KNIGHT (Gally).—An Architectural Tour in Normandy, ... 8vo, London, 1836
LANGLOIS (Eustache H.)—Stalles de la Cathedrale de Rouen (13 Copperplates), . Rouen, 1838
COCHET (Jean B. Desiré).—Les Églises de l'Arrondissement du Havre (12 Lithographs), ... 2 vols. 8vo, Havre, 1846
COCHET (Jean B. Desiré).—Les Églises de l'Arrondissement de Dieppe (10 Plates), 2 vols. 8vo, Dieppe, 1846
Do. Les Églises de l'Arrondissement d'Yvetôt (Woodcuts), 2 vols. 8vo, Paris, 1852
HIPPEAU (Ch.)—St. Etienne de Caen (l'Abbaye aux Hommes), . . . 8vo, Caen, 1855
CAUMONT (Arcisse de).—Statistique routière de la Basse Normandie, . 8vo, Paris, 1855
TREBUTIEN (G. S.)—Caen: Précis de son Histoire et ses Monuments, . . . 8vo, Caen, 1855
MUSGRAVE (George Musgrave).—A Ramble through Normandy,. . . 8vo, Lond. 1855
DION (A. de Laurent), LASVIGNES (L.) et FLACHÂT (E.)—Cathedrale de Bayeux et la Reprise en sous-œuvre de la tour centrale (25 Copperplates), . . 4to, Paris, 1861
RICKMAN (T.)—Tour in Normandy, 25th vol. *Archæologia*. . . . 8vo, London, 1770-1862
RUPRICH-ROBERT (V.)—L'Église St. Trinité (l'Abbaye aux Dames) et l'Église St. Etienne (l'Abbaye aux Hommes) à Caen (Engravings on Wood), . . 8vo, Caen, 1864
MERY (E.) et COCHET (J. B. D.)—Plan et Description de la Ville de Dieppe au XIV° siècle, 4to, Dieppe, 1865
JOLIMONT (F. T. de).—Les Principaux Édifices de la Ville de Rouen en 1525, dessinés à cette epoque . . . reproduits en facsimile, et publies avec Notes par F. de J., ... 8vo, Paris, 1846-67
*CAUMONT (Arcisse de).—Statistiques Monumentales de Calvados, . . . 8vo, Paris, 1846-67
BOUET (G.)—Analyse Architecturale de l'Abbaye de St. Etienne de Caen (Plates), . 8vo, Caen, 1868
BULLETIN MONUMENTALE, Normandy. Edited by Arcisse de Caumont, . . 8vo, Caen, 1834-1873

GENERAL WORKS CONTAINING REFERENCES TO NORMAN BUILDINGS.

GENTLEMAN'S MAGAZINE, 1809-10.—Controversy on the Origin of Gothic Architecture between Dr. Whittington, Architect Amateur, and Dr. Milner, 8vo, Lond. 1809-1810
QUARTERLY REVIEW, 1821.—Review of Books relating to Normandy, . . 8vo, London, 1821
CAUMONT (Arcisse de).—Histoire Sommaire de l'Architecture du Moyen Age, 8vo, Caen, 1834
Do. Cours d'Antiquités Monumentales, with atlas folio, 8vo, Paris and Caen, 1830-11
CHAPUY (N. F.)—Le Moyen Age Monumentale et Archæologique (240 Plates in lithog.), fol. 1843-46
RAMÉE (Daniel).—Histoire Générale de l'Architecture (Woodcuts), . . 8vo, Paris, 1860
PARKER (J. H.)—Abbey Churches of Caen. Gentlemen's Magazine, June, 1863, . 8vo, London, 1863
Do. Do. Transactions of the Royal Institute of British Architects (Plates), 1862-63-64, ... 4to, Lond. 1862-64
MURRAY'S Handbook for Travellers in France, ... 8vo, London, 1864
*FERGUSSON (J.), D.C.L., F.R.S.—History of Architecture in all Countries from the Earliest Times to the Present Day (many Wood Engravings), . . 8vo, London, 1865
CASSELL'S Topographical Guides (Normandy), ... 8vo, London, 1865
JOANNE (Adolphe L.)—Collection des Guides Joannes, ... 12mo, Paris, 1866
*VIOLLET LE DUC (E.M.)—Dictionnaire Raisonné de l'Architecture Française du XI° au XVI° siècle (many Wood Engravings), ... 10 vols. 8vo, Paris, 1858-68

ARCHITECTURAL ANTIQUITIES
OF NORMANDY.

A BRIEF REVIEW OF THE

CHARACTERISTICS OF CHRISTIAN ARCHITECTURE

IN NORMANDY.

FOR the purpose of obtaining a complete history and ample illustrations of the Architectural Antiquities of Normandy, it would be necessary to select various examples from all the different parts of the province. Almost every distinct department, as well as every building, presents some variations, either in the general design or subordinate architectural details; and although each of these may not be sufficient to mark a complete style or class, it constitutes an element which ought to be known and characterized, to complete the history of the style. In the present work we are only enabled to offer some evidences towards this history; we can merely bring forward a few examples, faithfully and geometrically delineated, as authentic documents to aid the critical historian, or as materials for the professional architect; each of whom will know how to apply them.

The accompanying illustrations are chiefly of Church Architecture, and mostly belong to an early class of buildings. There are a few of a late or decorated style, called the *Burgundian* in the *Quarterly Review*;[1] whilst some represent the domestic buildings dissimilar to anything in England, and which are certainly of singular characteristic features. The truly

[1 Review of books relating to Normandy. *Quarterly Review*, April to July, 1821.]

Norman specimens will be examined with much interest by the English antiquary, who seeks to deduce from them evidences either to confirm his own theories respecting the disputed distinctions between Saxon and Norman architecture, or to confute the theories of others.

Of the lancet, or first pointed style, our illustrations are not so numerous as could be wished; for the critical antiquary wants a mass of materials to exemplify and unfold the history of this *essential novelty and beauty* of architecture.[1] The origin and the progressive growth of the pointed style during nearly four centuries—its fanciful varieties and endless combinations—the latitude it gave to genius, and the numerous beauties of art and science which it has bequeathed to us, are so many claims on our curiosity and admiration. Whether it germinated in the East, in Italy, France, Normandy, Germany, or Britain, is a point not likely to be easily settled; nor is it worthy of jealous or envious contention. [It would take too long to trace the origin of the pointed arch, for the best account of which we refer the reader to a paper[2] by Mr. James Fergusson; a portion of which may be quoted here, as it sets at rest the question of the introduction of the pointed arch into Europe. Mr. Fergusson remarks, "With regard to the true Gothic, the view I take of the question is this: as every one knows, who is at all familiar with the Norman or round Gothic styles, the architects tried numberless expedients to get over the difficulties of using intersecting vaults with round arches; they stilted the smaller arches, depressed the larger ones; they tried quadripartite, sexapartite, and domical vaulting, and fifty other expedients, but without

---

[1] Mons. *Caumont* contends that the circular style was generally abandoned towards the end of the first half of the twelfth century, about 1140, and the pointed adopted. "Everything of the romance style disappeared, and the Gothic fashion was exclusively adopted." Our learned antiquary, however, qualifies this opinion, in a note, by saying, "The pointed style had existed at Coutances, Mortain, Seez, and Fécamp, ever since the eleventh century; but there are exceptions to the general rule; and Fécamp, for instance, is extremely heavy." I must venture to differ with Mons. Caumont respecting the Gothic fashion being *exclusively* adopted at the middle of the twelfth century; for we continually find the first pointed blended with the circular style in arches, mouldings, ornaments, &c., in England, and I am persuaded the same prevails in Normandy. See the upper parts of the towers at Bayeux Cathedral, the east end of Canterbury Cathedral, &c.

[2] Read before the Royal Institute of British Architects in 1849, and published in the *Builder* of June 23d and 30th of that year.]

ever attaining perfect or even satisfactory success. The curves of the ribs of the vaults were generally unpleasing, frequently waving and apparently crippled; and indeed the problem seemed almost insoluble. Still they seemed determined to persevere in the same path, rather than use the broken or pointed arch, in lieu of the graceful sweep of their unbroken curves.

"When things were in this state the Crusades took place; half Europe visited the East, and a Latin kingdom was established over the pointed-arch people of the Levant; and when they had thus become familiar with it, there can be little doubt but that they would perceive that so far from being necessarily ugly, the pointed arch could be worked into forms of as great beauty and elegance as the circular one; and had besides a lightness, and, for some purposes, an appropriateness the other did not possess. Once convinced of the fact, the problem was solved; the pilgrim architects returned from the Holy Land, and immediately applied this discovery to their western churches; once the prejudice was overcome they adopted it everywhere and in everything, and I need not add with what success.

"In adopting such a view of the question as this, there are two things to be guarded against: the first confounding the invention of the Gothic style with that of the pointed arch—a mistake too often fallen into; the former is a purely indigenous and native elaboration from Roman art, without any trace of copying or even imitation. The latter is a mere subordinate characteristic of that style, and not at all entitled to the rank it has hitherto assumed in the controversy.

"The other mistake is to assume that it was copied from the East for copying sake; the truth being, if we admit the above view, that the hint was given by the East, but nothing more; it was applied in Gothic buildings in a manner in which it had never been used in the East, and was so incorporated with and worked into the native style, that it soon lost all trace of its origin, and became as native as any other part of the true Gothic.

"Though, therefore, I do not think it can be denied but that the origin of the pointed arch is from the East, it must, I think, at the same time be admitted that all its appropriateness and all its beauty, as found in our mediæval cathedrals, is wholly due to the talent and ingenuity of our northern architects, who wrought it into those forms of beauty and grace which we all now so fully appreciate and so universally admire."]

It certainly behoves the historian of art to ascertain where and when the pointed style was systematized, and by whom and in what building it was employed throughout all the parts and members of the edifice. The adoption of an arch with a pointed apex, as at Malmesbury, in St. John's Church, Devizes, in Buildwas Abbey,[1] &c., does not prove that the architects were familiar with, or had introduced it as a member of an established style, but merely as a new feature in the formation of an opening in the wall, and adapted to the particular proportion of the edifice.[2] The lateral columns, the walls, the mouldings, continued nearly as before; and even the triforium openings, and windows of the aisles, as at Malmesbury and at Buildwas, were finished with semicircular heads. In the apsidal end of Canterbury Cathedral we recognize the pointed system or style, introduced not merely in the open arches between the centre and aisles, but in the slender shaft, with its capital and base, in the window, the buttress, the groining of the roof, &c. The circular arch was not then wholly abolished, nor were its analogous mouldings and details. The date of this part of the building is fortunately well authenticated (1176); and we have also very satisfactory evidence of successive and progressive improvements in the same style through the reigns of kings Richard I., John, and Henry III., in the cathedrals of York, Wells, Rochester, Salisbury, &c.

"It is in Normandy that the first pages of the architectural annals of this island (England) must be read. According to our most judicious antiquaries, no one structure, scarcely any one fragment, in Great Britain,

[1] See *The Architectural Antiquities of Great Britain*, where these buildings are represented and described.

[2] In the east end of Canterbury Cathedral it was judiciously made to suit the proportion of the intercolumns; at St. John's Church, Devizes, from the difference in the width of the tower at its two sides, one being much wider than the other, and yet the heights of the arches range together.

is now in existence that can be referred with *certainty* to the Saxon era.¹ Neither can we quote any architectural examples in Normandy of an earlier period than the eleventh century; at least if we wish to guide ourselves in our researches with any degree of satisfactory evidence or conjecture. The duchy of Normandy does not possess the monuments of Neustria.² The fury of the Northmen destroyed all the memorials both of Roman magnificence and of Christian piety, by which the province had been adorned, when they wrested it from the Carlovingian empire. Nought remained but scathed and mouldering walls, and these were afterwards lost in the edifices raised by the piety of the converted subjects of Rollo. A few insignificant remains—a tomb at *Lisieux*, a crypt at *Rouen*, a chapel at *Jumièges*, which probably ought to be dated before the Norwegian conquest, are of little moment in a general view of the subject, and do not connect themselves in the general series of specimens. It is useless to descant on relics of more dubious antiquity, which receive their date from untenable opinions; for the Norman archæologists, like our own, have often wrongly imagined that old age and ugliness must necessarily be synonymous. Thus, the abbey church of *St. Lo*, on account of its clumsy sculpture, has been considered as a temple of Isis, a deity who in France appears to claim all antiquarian estrays; and the church of *Bernières* is sometimes attributed by the Norman antiquaries to the old inhabitants of the 'Saxon shore,' though the marguilliers of the parish, with most reason, are satisfied that it owes its origin to Duke William."³

"The principal features of the Norman style are sufficiently familiar. Originating with the attempts which were successfully made to adapt the architecture of Rome to the uses of a Christian community, the order of which the Norman is merely a modification, acknowledges, in all its

[¹ Fergusson (*Hist. Arch.*, p. 844) qualifies this statement where he says: "There is no one instance of a complete Saxon church built before the Conquest; in some there is a tower, in others a fragment of walling, in others only a door or a window."]

[² Before the Norwegians, under Rollo, took possession of the north-western territory of France, at the commencement of the tenth century, it was called *Neustria*.

[³ It is doubtful whether any visible portion of the present church be older than the middle of the twelfth century; the tower, spire, and western porch date from the thirteenth century.]

varieties, the parent stock from which it sprang. Mr. Gunn proposes to distinguish this style by the name of the *Romanesque*.¹

" The Norman style being marked by some minor peculiarities which seem to distinguish it from the coeval modes of architecture used on the Continent, it might be the subject of conjecture whether the Norman buildings vary from their prototypes in consequence of any vestiges or reminiscences of the rude art of the first Norwegian settlers. Sacred structures were built in Scandinavia by the heathens. The flinty remains of the sacellum adjoining the cathedral church of *Upsala*, which is thought to have been dedicated to the sanguinary worship of the ' King of men,' are perforated by round Roman arches. Peringskiölld has given a representation of this edifice; but if anybody chooses to dispute its original destination, we shall not be inclined to fight very strenuously for the authenticity of Odin's Temple. We are not in the number of those who swear implicitly by the books of northern archæologists, who are usually fattened by erudition, at the expense of common sense and judgment."²

Religion has been invariably considered the most influential power of a nation: it is, therefore, to the edifices appropriated to the observance of its ordinances that we must look for specimens of the skill and taste of a people. The earliest churches, both in Normandy and in Britain, were extremely simple in their plan, scarcely differing from the basilicæ, or courts of justice, belonging to all the great cities of the Roman empire, many of which were, on the introduction of the religion of the Cross, converted into Christian churches, by order of the emperor Constantine. These basilicæ had their porticoes within the building—in that respect differing from the temples, which had them without, and consequently exposed to the weather,—and the end porticoes, in their width, were confined to the dimensions of the centre or oblong square of the building. The principal entrance was at one end, and the other was generally terminated in a semicircular form. In this plan are observable all the features of the early or primeval Christian churches. In the body of the basilica we distinctly trace the nave and aisles, in the chief entrance we recognize our west end, and in the termination our semicircular apse.

[¹ A term since generally adopted.]   ² *Quarterly Review*, June, 1821.

CHARACTERISTICS OF CHRISTIAN ARCHITECTURE.   7

In those places where the Romans had established themselves,[1] and erected houses or temples, we find that their peculiar brick was made use of, and specimens of these may now be seen in the crypt of the church of St. Gervais at Rouen, which some consider to be altogether of Roman workmanship. The masonic construction was also imitated. The masonry of the walls at *Vindomi* (Silchester), *Verulamium* (St. Alban's), and *Camalodunum* (Colchester)—stations established by the Romans—appears to have been disposed in a zigzag or herring-bone direction: and similar walls occur in the Norman churches of Anisy, Perriers, St. Matthieu, St. Croix at St. Lo, and St. Hildebert at Gournai. Others of the like kind are to be found in England, in the castles of Colchester, Corfe, Tamworth, &c. M. de Caumont, a French antiquary, speaking of the works of the Romans, says, that when they employed flat or rough stones they arranged them diagonally, and sloped in each alternate tier to the right and left;[2] but when they made use of cut stones they laid them horizontally; and we may remark, that the latter were small, and nearly of the same size. We also observe that the stones are sometimes disposed so as to resemble a chess-board; as at Ver, Mouen, the Abbaye aux Dames, Caen; tower of Steyning Church, Sussex, &c.

The extreme solidity of the materials, and the almost total absence of ornament, induce us to believe that the only aim of the architects was to erect edifices that should last for many ages; as at the church of Léry, near Pont de l'Arche, the interior of which is remarkable for those qualities.[3] They also appear to have been fearful of weakening the lateral

[1] It was far from being uncommon to find the edifices of that people mutilated and destroyed to furnish materials for new buildings;—metals were melted down, marbles were torn away, capitals and bases separated from their shafts and entablatures, &c. And this is not a subject of wonder, when we find that the senate of Rome had set the example, by plundering the ancient buildings for the decoration of the Triumphal Arch of Constantine. [2 Herring-bone masonry.]

[3] A double row of pillars and arches separate the body of the church into three parts of unequal width, and another arch of greater span divides it from the chancel. The arches are in every instance devoid of mouldings, the capitals altogether without ornamental sculpture of any description, and the pillars without bases—[a peculiarity confined to the ancient Grecian Doric, in classic architecture.] Indeed, the pillars are nothing more than rounded piers; and they are not less remarkable for their proportions than for their simplicity, their diameter being equal to full two-thirds of their height. These are in windows in the nave; but a series of statues adorn each side, resting on brackets between the arches.—Cotman, *Arch. Antiq. of Normandy*, vol i. pl. xlvi.

walls by piercing them for windows of any considerable dimensions, as we find the latter are but few, and those only narrow openings, of an oblong form. Their apses were also plain, as we may judge from the semicircular terminations of the church of Querqueville, near Cherbourg: and the apertures which were caused by the scaffolding were left, as appears throughout the whole of the body of Anisy Church, where, it is very remarkable, they are edged with freestone. The inconveniences consequent upon the narrow single-light openings must have compelled succeeding architects to provide for more light. Accordingly we notice, that the windows, from being narrow externally, expanded in width through the whole thickness of the wall, and formed a comparatively wide embrasure within. Normandy presents many specimens of the long and narrow semicircular-headed windows—resembling in size the lancet ones of the pointed style—in the short, square tower of St. Michael's Church, Vaucelles; and the examples are numerous of long cylindrical columns at small intervals, with small semicircular arches, and low massive cylinders supporting wider arches.

About the latter part of the ninth, or the commencement of the tenth century,[1] it is highly probable that the use of bells gave occasion to the first and most considerable alteration that was made in the general plan of our churches, by the necessity it induced of having strong and high-raised *towers* for their reception. These from being necessary soon became ornamental, and a lofty and light form was given to them, which was calculated to inspire those sentiments of awe which usually accompany admiration and surprise. About the same period

---

[1] I am aware that M. Caumont, in his *Essays on the Religious Architecture of Normandy*, adduces a passage from Anastas. Biblioth. in Vita Steph. III., proving the erection of a tower in the *eighth* century by that pope to the Church of St. Peter, to contain bells; but it was not till the period assigned above that the use of towers became indispensable, from the size of the bells. Mr. Whitaker, in his *Ancient Cathedral of Cornwall*, vol. ii. 152, and Mr. Faulkner, in his *History of Kensington*, have entered into ample dissertations on the origin and history of towers, bells, &c. [M. Viollet le Duc, in his *Dictionnaire Raisonné*, points out that no bells of any great size were cast before the twelfth century, and that previous to that epoch small belfries on the gable ends would have amply sufficed to hold the then comparatively small bells. He is inclined, therefore, to look upon these strong and lofty towers as emblems of the feudal power of the cathedral and abbeys, or of the richness and importance of the towns, and notices that it is principally in those countries where the secular

the churches began to be built in the form of a cross, a plan materially tending to heighten the general effect of the whole edifice, and which continued throughout the era in which the pointed style prevailed.

[*Eleventh and Twelfth Centuries.*]—In the eleventh century a new and most interesting era in the history of architecture commenced, for in it and the following century the Norman style may be said to have attained nearly to the summit of its grandeur: it will therefore deserve our serious and minute investigation. During this period the plan of the churches differed but little from those of the preceding century, being that of a cross, with the transepts extending north and south, and the east end marked by the semicircular-ending, or apse. The principal entrance was at the west end of the nave, and a tower was usually raised on each side of it, to coincide with and terminate the aisles. Another tower was frequently placed at the intersection of the cross, where it added to the solidity by pressing on the centre, against which the walls and arches abutted. The form of the towers was square, and they were pierced by semicircular arches more or less narrow, and variously distributed, sometimes duplicated, at others intersected; and again with two smaller arches within a larger one. About the latter part of the eleventh century, during the reign of William I. of England, the towers became larger in their square, more lofty, and had a proportionate degree of enrichment, being completely adorned on each side with two or three ranges, one above another, of small arcades,[1] of shallow depth, and sometimes interlacing each other to the number of twenty; thus producing an agreeable effect of richness and relief. Sometimes round towers are found, as at Tankerville; these were joined

feudalism had raised its most important castles that the cathedrals and abbeys, and later on the villages, erected their numerous and magnificent towers. M. Viollet le Duc suggests also that these towers were erected as a means of defence, and hence their position over the western doors; and that the raising of the bells into them was a matter of secondary importance only. (See article "Cloches," vol. iii. p. 286.)]

[1] Similar decorations are observable on the exterior of the body of the church. Thaon Church has a series of twenty-nine arches, every sixth of which, from the westward, is narrower than the rest, and pierced with a window. The surface of the blank ones is cut into squares, which are alternately depressed. Examples occur at the abbey churches of Tewkesbury and St. Albans, &c.

to the edifice, and the most ancient are comparatively low, whilst the pyramidal roofs that surmount them are stunted as at Ver.

The buttresses present the same appearance at the church of Fontaine le Henri; and they are occasionally decorated with angle-shafts, though this generally indicates that the work is late.¹ Cylindrical buttresses are occasionally observed. At the church of Cheux, on the north side of the east end, is one; and on the southern side of the round tower² of Tankerville, one runs nearly to the top of the first story.

The western entrances were, in the commencement of the eleventh century, very plain, with the exception of the principal doorways, the archivolts of which were enriched with numerous ornaments, of greater or less elaboration, according to the splendour of the building and the imagination of the architect. The church of St. Georges de Bocherville,³ "the most genuine and the most magnificent specimen of the circular style in Upper Normandy," has a doorway with as many as five orders of mouldings, all highly worked, and presenting almost every pattern commonly found in such parts of Norman buildings. According to Mr. D. Turner, Normandy does not contain a richer arch than this; but in England numbers are to be found, even in obscure parish churches, which are equal to it, if not superior in richness.⁴ At Bieville and Perriers there are square-headed doorways, the lintels of which are cut into the shape of pediments, with semicircular relieving arches. That at Bieville is surrounded by only a single, flat, and plain moulding, whilst the one at Perriers displays some pleasing decorations. We frequently find that where a square-headed doorway occurs under an

[¹ The broad shallow buttress is one of the chief characteristics of Norman work. It was doubtless derived from the pilasters of classic architecture, and, like them, seems to have been used more for the purposes of decoration than for any actual support to the walls. This is especially the case in all the Lombard churches and in those on the Rhine. The Norman buttress is generally not divided into stages, but continues of the same breadth and depth from bottom to top, and either dies into the wall with a slope just beneath the corbel-table (*Plate V.*) or assists to carry it (*Plate XIX.*)]

² The round towers are more properly the productions of a century later. There is one at St. Ouen, Rouen, built by Abbot William Balot in 1126.

[³ Illustrated very fully in Nodier's *Voyages Pittoresque de France* (*Normandie*) and in Cotman's *Architectural Antiquities of Normandy.*]

⁴ At Iffley, Tutbury, Ely, Malmesbury, &c.

arch, the tympanum or intermediate space between the arch and the stone lintel is filled with bas-reliefs, rudely carved, as at Marigny and Colville, in the district of Bayeux; Urville, in the department of La Manche; and Bully and Cambe, in the district of Caen. Sometimes, but the examples are very rare, we find arched doors without columns —though the early windows are commonly so—and adorned with ornaments the whole height.[1] At Frenouville, Busly, Plessis-Grimoult, is a kind of doorway, which, according to M. de Caumont, has round the arches one or more rows of stone, generally cut in the form of a wedge, and arranged so as to be jointed one within the other. These are commonly decorated by a profusion of delicately sculptured stars [known as "Stars of Bethlehem"]. frequently with undulating points. Specimens of similar work may be seen in the churches of the pointed style, and in the monuments of the thirteenth and fourteenth centuries.

The walls, from the western towers to the transept, form a parallelogram on plan, which is divided by ranges of arches into three unequal compartments, the nave and two aisles. The columns, or piers, and the semicircular arches producing these divisions, are more or less ornamented, according to the antiquity of the edifice and the importance of the building. At the abbey church of Jumieges the arches alternately spring from round pillars and from square piers, with semicylindrical columns affixed to each of their sides; and at Pavilly they are supported by clustered columns, with unadorned capitals and enormous hexagonal bases. Sometimes we observe duplicated columns, that is, two isolated columns rising from one base, and crowned by one capital, as in the Abbaye aux Hommes at Caen, at Canterbury, &c. The columns of the era of which we are treating had no fixed proportions, being either heavy and short, or very tall and light, and some rising to a considerable height: they are all of equal thickness from top to bottom, and in general have a sort of plinth for a base, sometimes only a few inches

---

[1] The inner archivolt of the western entrance at Foullebec is carved into flower-work, whilst the outer moulding has the plain embattled fret of considerable size, and some grotesque carving, besides two sculptural pieces, representing the lamb and flag, and a man on an ass—probably our Saviour riding through Jerusalem.

high, and at others one or two feet: but this was varied in different ages. The base is sometimes composed of a plinth and a torus: and in one or two instances may be seen a near approximation to the Attic base.

The capitals of the columns appear to be extremely rude imitations of the various orders of classic architecture.[1] The most ancient are miserably executed Tuscan and Doric, grotesquely carved; but the Corinthian and Composite are the most commonly imitated: the rarest is that of the Ionic. The church of St. Georges de Bocherville has a pleasing variety of specimens; for we there find the receding abacus and richly sculptured foliage of the Corinthian, as well as a mixture of grotesque. In the church of the Holy Trinity, at Caen, the capitals are ornamented with rams' heads, the horns of which form the volutes, curling out from beneath the abacus. From the rich display of diversified capitals to be found at St. Georges de Bocherville, St. Hildebert at Gournay, &c., we are enabled to form some idea of the extent to which the caprice and imagination of the architects led them. Some of these represent gryphons, lacs d'amour, grotesque heads, or monsters with their heads turned behind them, and biting their tails, some of which are cloven towards the end. Besides the chimeras, serpents, dragons, and all the inexplicable creations of the imaginative fancy, we discern some allegorical figures and subjects from religious history, the most esteemed of all adorned capitals. The arches springing from these columns have sometimes very enriched archivolts. As the *mouldings* which serve to decorate them are similar to those employed in the arches of the western and other entrances, and in the enriched windows, we have thrown into a note a list of many of them, with references to the churches where they are to be met with.[2]

[1] The capitals of the columns remaining at St. Sanson, we are informed by Mr. Joseph Woods, resemble those of the temple of Bacchus at Teos. [There are none published of this temple which resemble those of St. Sanson, but similar examples are found in the temples of Minerva Polias at Priene, and Apollo Didymaeus near Miletus; with this difference, however, that the Greek examples are capitals of square piers; those of St. Sanson, of circular columns. In Pompeii also are many similar capitals.]

[2] The most common ornament is that of the *chevron*, or *zigzag*, which seems to have been the earliest used, and latest abandoned (see *Plate I.*) When there are many rows of them they are called, according

Above the arches, between the nave and aisles, usually runs a string-course, separating the lower arches from those of the next story, called the triforium, the arches of which are sometimes of nearly the same width as those below, though less in height, as at the abbey church of Jumieges, where they are devoid of either archivolts or mouldings. They seldom or ever were pierced with windows, but generally formed a kind of communication with the tower and roof of the edifice. They are subject to all the varieties which distinguish the Norman arches, as well in distribution as in plan and decoration. Above the triforium was a range of windows called the clerestory, which are in general devoid of pillars, are unadorned, and narrower externally than they are within.

The choir and sacrarium usually terminate with a semicircular apse; but instances occur, as at Fontaine le Henri, and at Thaon, of square east ends. The churches of the Holy Trinity and of St. Nicholas at Caen (*Plate XIX*.), and at Cheux, may be considered as good specimens of the general features of the exterior of these apses, being divided by slender cylindrical pillars into several compartments, and by string-courses into three stories, the basement one occupied by a range of small arcades, the heads of which are hewn out of a single stone, and the others

to the numbers, double, triple, quadruple, zigzags, &c. A specimen of the chevron, disposed in a triple row, occurs at the church of St. Giles, at Evreux, now used as a stable. Their angles are more or less acute; and sometimes we see two rows of zigzags with the angles opposite one another (*Plate XXIII.*) This is called by M. de Caumont the *zigzag contre zigzag*. A specimen may be seen in Bayeux Cathedral (*Plate XXVIII.*) The *embattled fret* is formed by a single round moulding, traversing the face of the arch, making its returns, and crossing at right angles, so forming the intermediate spaces into squares, alternately open above and below (see *Plates VI.* and *XVII.*) In England we frequently observe a *triangular fret*, where the same kind of moulding at every return forms the side of an equilateral triangle, and incloses the intermediate space in that figure. *Billets* resemble a cylindrical piece of wood, sawed into many pieces of equal length (see *Plates XII.* and *XVII.*) The *nail-head* resembles the heads of great nails, driven in at regular distances. This is so rare an ornament for the string-course in Normandy, that Mr Cotman recollects no other instance of it than in the church of Léry, near Pont de l'Arche. The *hatched moulding* appears to have its origin from the circumstance of the workmen making indents in the mortar with their trowels, and is accordingly a very general ornament of the string-course. *Nebules*, or undulating lines. Of the *dog-tooth* a specimen exists at the church of St. Georges de Bocherville. *Cable*, or twisted mouldings (*Plate XVII.*) A line of *quatrefoils* may be seen at the church of St. Giles, at Evreux. This ornament, so exceedingly common in the pointed style, is said to be met with on this one Norman building only. Birds' heads and beaks were sometimes placed round the arches; and a great variety of foliage, besides many indescribable combinations, likewise appear.

pierced by windows, variously diversified; the whole terminated by roofs of very high pitch: the *corbel tables*[1] are grotesquely sculptured. The choir of Cheux is remarkable for being wider than the nave. The portion east of the tower is of three distinct parts, unequal in size, the central being the narrowest, but all of the same height, and each lateral one exactly equalling in its width the length of the transept to which it is attached, and thus, also, the choir and transepts collectively form nearly a square, except that to the end of the middle compartment is attached a semicircular apse.

From the north and south sides, between the nave and choir, and producing a cruciform arrangement of plan, project the transepts, at the northern and southern extremities of which chapels are placed across. The general features of these transverse chapels (which were vaulted at the level of the aisle vault, and usually dedicated to some saint) accorded with the style of the nave, when of the same era; but at the abbey churches of Fécamp, St. Stephen at Caen (*Plate II.*), and Cérisy, in the cathedral of Séez, and at St. Georges de Bocherville, the transept chapels are separated by screens, by means of which Mr. Cotman considers that the architects intended that the aisle of the nave should receive apparent length from the columns which form the screen ranging in a line with the outer walls of the aisles. To the eastern end of these transverse chapels it was customary to affix small semicircular chapels, as at St. Nicholas at Caen, St. Taurin at Evreux, &c., in Normandy, and at Canterbury, Norwich, and elsewhere, in England.

[*Thirteenth Century.*]—The circular style, which may be said to have reached its maturity in Normandy about the middle of the twelfth century, was destined during the thirteenth to give way to a new phase more adapted to the immense development of religious rites. But this

[1] This feature was derived originally from the jutting out or projection of the joists of the roof underneath the cornice or eaves. They were carved and ornamented with a great variety of patterns, as heads of monsters, gryphons, birds, &c. The most ancient are highly projecting, and are surmounted by a heavy flat cornice, and others of subsequent date support small arcades (see *Plate XX.*) The cornice over the corbels is often adorned with zigzags, billets, &c. At first, like the corbels, they projected considerably, but gradually diminishing, they were superseded by the light parapets of the pointed style.

was not effected without a struggle, and was done neither simultaneously nor uniformly; for we frequently find that in the buildings of the end of the twelfth century the two styles are variously intermixed. When the pointed arch began to be introduced, the ornaments which had been used to decorate the archivolts of the semicircular arches were retained and applied to the new ones; as at the abbey church of Jumieges, where are frets, cables, clustered columns, ornamented capitals, pointed arches, &c.[1] Another illustration of the intermixture of styles appears at the west end of St. Peter's Church at Lisieux, where are windows composed of two small pointed arches resting on a cylindrical column in the centre, and inclosed by a larger arch resting on clustered columns with Norman sculptured capitals.

At the beginning of the thirteenth century the circular arch and cylindrical column seem wholly to have been disused, and the pointed arch and slender shafts substituted in their places. These shafts were clustered, and consisted of a larger one in the centre, with others either wholly detached or separated in the shafts, and joined in the capitals and bases. They were variously adorned with sculpture.[2] The vaulting, or webs, in the early pointed style were generally made of chalk, or soft stone, for lightness; but the arches and principal ribs were formed of more durable materials. The greatest distinguishing marks of all eras are the windows. In those of the thirteenth century we observe them long, narrow, sharp-pointed, and decorated on the inside and outside with small shafts. The order and disposition of the windows varied in some measure according to their position. Thus in the clerestory, or uppermost story of a building, we should find a triplet, or three windows grouped together, the centre one being higher than those on each side. The story beneath, or triforium, would have two within the

[1 This admixture of styles is well illustrated in the choir of the Abbaye aux Hommes, which, erected at the close of the twelfth or beginning of the thirteenth century, displays its transition features in the decoration of the pointed arch ribs, with the Norman chevron or zigzag ornament (*Plate IX.*) The same feature is found in the choir of Canterbury.]

[2] Some of the clustered columns are annulated, that is, fixed or tied together in the middle by rings, as at Bayeux, St. Stephen's at Caen, &c., and in Westminster Abbey Church, Salisbury Cathedral, the Temple Church, &c., in our own country.

same space; and the lowest only one window, usually divided by a pillar or rather mullion, and often ornamented on the top with a trefoil, single rose, or some such simple decoration. The walls were less in thickness than in the circular style, but were strengthened by buttresses of much greater projection, which terminated in pinnacles adorned with crockets, and finished with a handsome flower of four petals, called a finial.

The *distinctive character* of the architecture of this early era lies in its simplicity; but when ornaments were introduced, they were usually bold and well-executed—especially the foliated capitals of pillars, and the scrolls of foliage with which the spandrils of the arches were sometimes filled. Towards the latter end of this century the pillars became more solid, the lights of the windows were enlarged, and the slender detached shafts in a great measure laid aside. The four-sided pyramid, which usually terminated the towers during the continuance of the circular style, was superseded by the octagonal spire, the base of which was relieved, and its beauty heightened, by the introduction of richly decorated pinnacles at each of the angles of the cornice of such towers.[1]

[*Fourteenth Century.*]—The church of *St. Ouen*, at Rouen, affords a most pleasing and perfect specimen of the more decorated style which prevailed in the fourteenth century. By examining the Plates of this edifice (*XXXVIII.-XLIII.*) we shall perceive flying-buttresses end in richly crocketed pinnacles, supported by shafts of unusual height. The triple tiers of windows seem to have superseded the solid wall-work of the building. The vaulting is more decorated than before; and the ribs are usually ornamented at their intersections with gilded orbs, carved heads, figures, and other sculptured work. The columns retained something of the general form already described, that is, an assemblage of small pillars or shafts; but these decorations were now not detached or separated from the body of the column or pier, but made part of it; and being closely united and wrought up together, formed one entire, firm, slender, and elegant column. The *windows* were now greatly enlarged, and divided into several lights by stone mullions, running into various ramifications above, [and forming what is now

[1 See notice of the spires of Normandy, page 22 *et seq.*]

CHARACTERISTICS OF CHRISTIAN ARCHITECTURE.   17

known as flamboyant tracery]; and more particularly the great eastern and western windows (which became fashionable about this time) took up nearly the whole breadth of the nave, and were carried up almost as high as the vaulting; and being set off with stained glass, of vivid colours, had a solemn and imposing appearance. [In fact generally, at this period the whole of the available space under the vault and between the clustered piers was occupied by windows filled with stained glass; showing how the architects of that day sought to diminish the size of the main supports of the building and to increase the space allotted to stained glass. The object of this is apparent: the climate of northern France not always rejoicing in the bright, clear atmosphere of more eastern climes, the interiors of these great cathedrals and churches would have appeared cold and gloomy were it not for the brilliant colours which the rays of light piercing through the stained glass spread throughout the church. The multiplication of rays of various colours had also the effect of increasing the apparent size of the building, so that this church of St. Ouen, for instance, though of comparatively moderate dimensions, appears as vast as a cathedral. (*Viollet le Duc*, vol. ix.)] Large *circular windows*, sometimes known by the name of rose-windows and marigold-windows, prevail in the Norman and French churches of the pointed style of the fourteenth century. Few among the cathedrals or conventual churches in France are without them; but in England the specimens are very few. In the church of St. Ouen these windows are more than commonly beautiful. That in the west front is fully delineated in *Plates XLII. XLIII.*; whilst another, in the northern transept, is almost as rich. Others in the cathedral church of Rouen are still more elaborate in their tracery.

The arches of doorways, of monuments, &c., were often very richly ornamented with foliage and crockets, and the pinnacles were enriched in the same manner. This elegant and peculiar ornament, the crocket, is prevalent during the whole of the pointed style. In the early part of the fourteenth century the arches were also frequently adorned with running foliated ornament in the hollow mouldings. (*Plate XLI.*)

A parapet of open quatrefoils runs round the aisles and body of the church of St. Ouen; and the centre tower, which is almost wholly composed of open arches and tracery, terminates, like the south tower of the cathedral, with an octangular crown of fleurs-de-lis. This armorial symbol of France, which in itself is a form of great beauty, was often introduced by the French architects of the middle ages amongst the ornaments of their edifices, and that with a very pleasing and satisfactory result.

[*Fifteenth Century.*]—The same style and manner of building prevailed during the early half of the fifteenth century, when it verged into a more florid description of architecture, which may be said to have led to its decadence. The ribs of the vaulting were divided into an infinite number of mouldings, issuing from the vaulting shafts, sometimes without capitals or imposts, and enriched with a profusion of sculpture, and with clusters of pendant ornaments. In this century, and in the beginning of the following, the bosses of the vaulted roofs were wrought into filagree, the work extending over the intersection of the ribs which are seen through its reticulation. The wall surfaces were also very frequently covered with abundance of rich tracery, giving them the appearance of embroidery. The heads of the windows were more richly ornamented with tracery; and the jambs were formed into niches or tabernacles, with enriched canopies, the soffits of which were minutely adorned with filagree work. The large windows were usually divided by two bold mullions into three parts, which were again subdivided into smaller compartments. Indeed, the architecture of this century lost all its religious grandeur and sublime solemnity; but what it lost in that respect, it gained in richness and exuberance of ornament. Every part of the edifice, however minute, was loaded with delicate mouldings: and while we may admire the fancy displayed in frittering the surface of a building into such toyish decoration, we cannot but regret the extinction of that pleasing simplicity which alone is in accordance with propriety and good taste. [In secular architecture the forms of the arches became more and more obtuse, till they were in some cases almost flat, the four-centred arch, which abounds in our Tudor style, being rarely found, otherwise the characteristics of the two styles in France and England

CHARACTERISTICS OF CHRISTIAN ARCHITECTURE. 19

are very similar. The introduction of the ogee arch label over windows and doors in secular and ecclesiastical work dates also from this period.]

Of the churches at *Coutances, Lisieux, Séez*, and others, in which the early pointed style prevails in its genuine simplicity, and evincing its lofty and elegant characteristics, we regret that we are unable to offer the antiquarian architect any engraved examples. He will find, however, some interesting illustrations of parts of all these edifices in Mr. Cotman's valuable work, as well as judicious essays on the ages and styles of each. "The church of Séez," says Mr. Turner, "may be compared in its architecture with those of Coutances and Lisieux; they are unlike, indeed, but by no means different. Severe simplicity characterizes Lisieux: Coutances is distinguished by elegance, abounding in decoration; Séez, at the same time that it unites the excellencies of both, can rival neither in those which are peculiarly its own. In the interior it exhibits a series of noble lofty arches: below, the moresque ornament, like those at Bayeux and Coutances, in the spandrils; the double lancet arches of the triforium placed in triplets; and the larger pointed arches above, arranged two or three together, and increased with arches of the Norman form, though not of the Norman style."[1]

In the middle of the fifteenth century, and at the commencement of the sixteenth, an admixture of the Italian with that of the florid Gothic style produced a somewhat inconsistent and not altogether harmonious style of architecture, which Mr. Dawson Turner has designated by the appellation of the Burgundian.[2] This almost distinctive species of architecture seems to have been wholly employed in domestic buildings. Specimens must therefore be sought for among that class of edifices; and we accordingly find some very fine illustrations in the mansion of *Château Fontaine le Henri* (*Plates LXXI.-LXXIII.*), in the *Palais de Justice* at Rouen (*Plates XLIX.-LIV.*), and in the *Hôtel de Bourgtheroulde* in the Place de la Pucelle, at Rouen (*Plates LV. LVI.*) This last is the

[1] *Architectural Antiquities of Normandy*, vol. ii. p. 125.
[2] So called because supposed to have originated in the dominions of Philip the Good. No distinct example of it can be dated anterior to his reign, and buildings bearing its characteristics are found in all the states which were united under his authority. Its peculiar features are also displayed in Philip's palace at Dijon.

richest specimen, being entirely divided into compartments by slender and lengthened buttresses and pillars. The intervening spaces are filled with basso-relievos, some of which are rich and fanciful and represent the labours of the field and of the vineyard. Here also, though of much later date, is a series of bas-reliefs, executed in marble tablets, displaying the royal interview between Henry VIII. and Francis I. on the Field of the Cloth of Gold (*Champ du Drap d'Or*). The windows are in general square-headed, and divided into four parts by a perpendicular stone munition and a transom, and are decorated with a series of plain mouldings, extending round all the four sides, and giving them the appearance of being in panel. Where pointed (generally in the upper stories), they are particularly rich, being finished with angular pediments supported by buttresses, terminating in pinnacles highly crocketed, and surmounted by bold finials. The tympana are commonly occupied by armorial bearings, and a range of foliage runs in the hollow of the arch mouldings.

Thus we have endeavoured to trace the progress of architecture in Normandy from its infancy to perfection, and from perfection to a species of enervated second childhood. With the gradual decline of the massive Norman, rose the beautiful pointed style, a description of architecture less understood by the French than by the English antiquaries, and of which Normandy presents some good specimens, though mostly far inferior in the taste and execution of the detail to some that might be cited in England.[1] We have seen the elegant assemblage of ornaments which the pointed style displayed in its height of grandeur; and we have had to contemplate, with feelings of regret and mortification, its barbaric fall into that inharmonious, disagreeable jumble of styles and

[1] A few portions of some English buildings resemble others in France—Canterbury choir, for instance; but no entire building is found in France which can be compared to one of entirely English design. In the arrangement of the structure, in the style of the ornaments, in the elevation, in the section, in the plan—in short, in some part or feature, a diversity will always be found, which, without destroying the genuine Gothic character, designates a specific class. The continental churches nearly all terminate in a semicircular or polygonal apse. Westminster, Canterbury, Tewkesbury, Norwich, &c., in England, are built on this plan, but English examples of this special feature are by no means numerous. The foreign churches have often four side aisles, and as the churches thus became very broad, the extremities of the transepts usually range within the walls of the side aisles, instead of projecting beyond them. Of such magnificence we have but few examples in England.

orders, which began to prevail, and seemed to satisfy the public taste, in the sixteenth century. Happy indeed was it for the credit of the country and for the fame of its artists, when Italian architecture, introduced with greater perfection, was released from the shackles of a debased taste, and allowed to claim its due place and its meed of praise. In the present day, though it is painful to observe the general want of refined taste, as well in England as on the Continent, it is gratifying to find that the science of architecture is making rapid strides, is becoming familiar to the enlightened few, and is considered a necessary part of the education of the man of taste and the scholar. With the following apposite remarks from the *Quarterly Review*, let us terminate this introductory essay.

"The Anglo-Norman style appears in its native country with slight variations. Generally speaking, the *Norman doorway* is less enriched than the English portal, though it is of larger dimensions; and the same remark applies to the other parts of the front of the edifice. The windows are larger. No building now exists with a flat bordered roof, as at Peterborough and St. Albans;[1] though it is possible that some may have thus been originally constructed. In such of the Norman buildings as bear the appearance of being built by the more scientific architects of the age, the arches spring from piers, except in the apses, and they are locked by a keystone. This construction shows that the architect did not forget the lessons of a better age. The *masonry* is always excellent; the stones seldom exceed a foot in length, with about a third of an inch of mortar in the joints. All ornaments composed of foliage, or of mathematical lines, are well sculptured; but the artist did not always succeed in the representation of animal life. Spires are not an uncommon feature in Norman architecture; we may instance the square pyramid at Vaucelles, and in the suburbs of Bayeux; they are well built of stone, and invariably carved into an imitation of shingles.

[1 The Abbaye aux Hommes had originally a wooden roof, a description of which, written by M. Bouet, will be found in the *Bulletin Monumentale* of the Society of Antiquaries, Normandy, vol. xxix.; and also in a paper read by Mr. J. H. Parker, Jan. 26, 1863, before the Royal Institute of British Architects, and published in their *Transactions* of the years 1862–63.]

"As we have no instance of the Norman spire in England, these examples are valuable. At St. Nicholas the roof is wholly of stone and the pitch is very high. Mr. Turner observes, 'that we have here the exact counterpart of the Irish stone-roofed chapels, the most celebrated of which, that of Cormac, in Cashel Cathedral, appears, from all the drawings and descriptions which I have seen of it, to be altogether a Norman building.'"

THE SPIRES OF NORMANDY.

Mr. J. H. Parker, in his paper on the Abbaye aux Hommes, Caen, already referred to, makes the following general observations on the spires of Normandy, while describing those of Caen.

It should be observed that in nearly all the spires in this district the surface of the stone is cut to imitate wooden shingles or tiles, a clear proof that there were earlier spires of wood from which these were copied; indeed there is little doubt that all the Norman towers either had or were intended to have spires of some kind. The frequent burning of the wooden spires, and the natural decay of the material in such an exposed situation, has caused them to disappear; and in England the towers have gradually been left with their square tops calling in vain for spires. In this part of Normandy, where the building stone is so abundant and so easily worked, stone spires were very generally introduced in place of the wooden ones.

I am very much inclined to believe that Europe is indebted to Caen and its neighbourhood for that very interesting feature in mediæval architecture—the Gothic spire of stone. I know of no other district in which we can trace such a series of steps leading up by a natural succession and progress to this object, as the pyramids which form a common termination of the church towers of this neighbourhood. Beginning with the very remarkable and curious low pyramid of Thaon (see *Plate XX*.), which may fairly be assigned to the end of the eleventh century, we can here readily trace the successive changes at intervals not exceeding ten years from each other, in a series gradually becoming more lofty, better executed, and evidently later in character, until we come first to the square spire, and then by a natural and easy transition to the octagonal spire with its groups of pinnacles and spire-lights (*lucarnes*) at the base. To begin then with Thaon; in this remarkable structure the surface is not made even in one gradual slope, as was afterwards the case, but the pyramid is built in a succession of steps with the angles chamfered off; and within the stones are not cut, but left rough and overhanging one another, like the Irish cairns and bee-hive houses; and at the base of the pyramid a large piece of timber was introduced, like the wall-plate on top of a wall, as if to bind the lower together, and make a secure base to construct the pyramid upon.—The next pyramid in date is probably that of Comornes, near Bayeux, which is a tall tower possessing some curious features of quite the beginning of the twelfth century or the end of the eleventh. The pyramid itself is low and very early-looking. It is built of ashlar, the upper part has been repaired, and has unfortunately had a window and a bell put on the top. The next which occurs to me is Basly, near Caen, which belongs to near the middle of the twelfth century, and Rosel, which follows very soon after. These are simple pyramids without any corner pinnacles; the latter has a round moulding on the angles, a finial, and spire-light.

Huppeau, near Bayeux, may come next. It is considerably taller than those that have gone before, but appears to be nearly if not quite as early. It has a large roll-moulding on the angles, and the surface is cut in imitation of shingles. At each of the four corners is a sort of rude large crocket, the lower edges of the pyramid resting upon a corbel-table, as is usually the case, and these corbels are very rudely carved, but the cutting is deep. Vaucelles, in the suburbs of Caen, has been repaired, but copied with tolerable fidelity, and belongs to this period. St. Loup at Bayeux, which has been engraved by Pugin (*Plate XXIII.*), is another very fine example of this class. St. Contest, near Caen, has also had the pyramid rebuilt in modern times, but faithfully copied, and may be classed here. Bons is a fine example of transitional character, which may be called either a very tall pyramid or a square spire; it has no corner pinnacles, but has lucarnes in the centre of each face.

Douvres may be taken next: it is octagonal, but very early, quite of transitional character, and stands on a tower of the same period. The small square spires at the east end of St. Stephen's, at Caen, have been already mentioned, and should perhaps come before Douvres. Ducy is a very elegant, lofty, octagonal spire, with square pinnacles, and is a little earlier than the western spires of St. Stephen's, Caen.

The spires of the Cathedral of Bayeux (*Plates XXV. XXVI.*) are so much of the same character as those of St. Stephen's. Caen (*Plate III.*), that they were probably building at the same time. They are not equally elegant, and the corner pinnacles are not so open, which gives them rather an earlier appearance. Secqueville has a fine spire of nearly the same character, possibly a little earlier, having no corner pinnacles, but it has lucarnes, and these correspond closely with the others.

Those of Bretteville, Bernières, and Langrune follow in this order, and bring us to about the middle of the thirteenth century. They are all admirable examples of elegant design and wonderfully light construction, and each is of itself a study for a young architect. After these come the unfinished spires of Norrey and Audrieu, which brings us to the end of the century. Norrey is one of the most beautiful of this district of beautiful churches; it is often said to be copied from St. Stephen's, Caen, but it is almost an exact copy of the Cathedral of Bayeux on a small scale, quite a little model of a cathedral. It was intended to be made far more rich on the exterior, but was never completed. The small portions that are finished are exquisite pieces of Gothic detail and carving, but it is of considerably later date, near the end of the century. The spire was never completed, but it is carried above the top of the pinnacles, which are finished, and show what was intended to be. At the east end a whimsical fancy has been introduced; the two apsidal chapels have each a half spire carried up for a roof, so that they look as if the two had been split asunder, and ought to be joined together again. The effect is very bad, and even ludicrous, and this seems to show that when the architect deviated from his model he was not to be trusted, although the workmen possessed wonderful skill.

This brings us to the spires of the fourteenth century, of which St. Peter's, at Caen (*Plates XXXV. XXXVI.*), is the favourite type, and which is commonly quoted as the perfection of a spire, although some prefer the earlier type, of which St. Stephen's affords the most perfect example. The spire of St. Saviour's, at Caen, would rank very high if it were not so near to St. Peter's, to which it is not quite equal."

ON THE ORIGIN AND DEVELOPMENT OF VAULTING.

BY THE EDITOR.

The history of the transition from Norman to Pointed architecture would scarcely now be considered complete without some special reference to those magnificent vaults, the development of which gave so great an impetus to the style, and constituted in fact its chief characteristic.

As in all perfected architectural styles, the method of covering in or vaulting over large interiors will be found to have given the key-note to the formation of each style, so in the vaults of the middle ages may we trace the great development of the principal features of Gothic architecture.

The researches which have been made by M. Viollet le Duc and M. de Caumont in France, and by Professors Willis, Whewell, and G. G. Scott, and Messrs. J. Fergusson and J. H. Parker in England, and the books and essays that have appeared since the first publication of Pugin's *Normandy*, have placed the subject on an entirely different footing from that laid down in the first quarter of this century, and the theories of Dr. Milner, Whittington, and others, have been altogether set aside. There is no phase in the history of pointed architecture fraught with more interest to the student than that which is displayed in the introduction of ribbed vaulting; and seeing that in the churches of the Abbaye aux Hommes and the Abbaye aux Dames, the cathedral of Bayeux, and the church of St. Ouen at Rouen (all of which are illustrated in this volume), will be found four of the principal varieties of stone vaults, we have thought the subject worthy of a separate chapter.

The earliest system to which it is necessary to revert is that of the simple barrel-vault of the Romans, with or without intersections. These were constructed, as M. Viollet le Duc has shown, on somewhat similar principles to the Gothic vault;[1] that is to say, that at certain distances were erected centres, planks being laid between; over these centres were voussoirs of bricks or tiles, placed on end, forming ribs, the spaces between being filled with mortar and light rubble work, and occasionally a single layer of flat bricks or tiles underneath; the whole surface being afterwards covered with stucco, and painted or decorated with mosaics. No great difficulty was experienced in the formation of the quoins of these intersecting barrel-vaults, so long as the latter were of the same diameter and with their springing on the same level; when, however, as was often the case in the great halls of the Roman baths, the main vault was intersected by smaller ones with either the apex or the springing at a different level, the quoin or intersecting angle became a double curve, and exceedingly awkward to construct, presenting also disagreeable forms to the eye.

The introduction of the rib, no longer to be hidden from view as in the Roman vault, but as a primary and leading feature on which the main vault itself was to be laid, and from which it was to take its form, constituted a new solution of the problem, and the chief and leading characteristic of Gothic architecture. The advantages of this introduction were twofold; first, it enabled the builder to erect his arched ribs on a simple system of centering in one plane, in most cases probably to do away with centering altogether for the main vault or arch; and secondly,

[1] "Si l'on prend la peine d'analyser ces larges voûtes romaines, berceaux, voûtes d'arêtes, coupoles, on constate que ces surfaces courbes, en apparence uniformes et homogènes, sont formées d'une suite de nerfs et même de cellules de brique dont les intervalles sont remplis par un blocage composé de pierres légères et de mortier. Ainsi pour fermer une très-grande voûte, suffisait-il de poser un certain nombre de cintres de charpente, relativement restreint et d'une force mediocre, de les reunir par une forme de planches sur lesquelles la voûte était construite." —*Dictionnaire Raisonné*, vol. ix. p. 105).

it concentrated with more accuracy the thrust of the whole vault in certain well defined directions.

It is true that in the Pantheon and Roman baths the masonry which counterbalanced the thrusts of their vaults was grouped in masses at the most important points, and so far corresponded to the comparatively thin walls, with occasional buttresses and flying-buttresses of the middle ages; but the Romans regarded these constructive expedients as unpleasant necessities, and therefore either carefully hid them from view, as in the Pantheon, or, as in their vaulted temples, made use of pilasters and columns, which were intended to be looked upon as decorative, whilst they were really constructive features, though not intended for the purpose to which they were thus applied. The mediæval architects, on the contrary, frankly accepted the buttress, and invented new forms for it, which were not only in accordance with the constructive requirements it was called upon to fulfil, as a resistance to thrust, but were graced with all those decorative features which constitute its chief beauty.

As far back as the first and second century we find the simple transverse rib used by the Romans, in the vaulting of their piscinæ; its adoption, however, did not become general till the tenth century; and even after that date the Roman vault without ribs was still employed, as seen in the crypt of the Abbaye aux Dames at Caen (*Plate XIV.*), dating from 1066. In the same church, but later on, we find the side aisles and choir vaulted in square compartments, with transverse but no diagonal ribs; and there is every reason to believe that the aisles of the Abbaye aux Hommes at Caen were vaulted over in like manner. Up to the twelfth century no attempt had been made to vault over the naves or transepts of those early Norman churches, and they were, as in England, covered with wooden roofs; when therefore the experiment was first made in the Abbaye aux Hommes, that great change was effected to which we have before alluded; in the place of the Roman method, in which circular barrel-vaults were employed, the quoin or groin being determined by the intersection of these vaults, an entirely new system was introduced; the ribs were erected first, being circular or elliptical in form, and between and resting on them were light stone vaults or webs, which derived their shape mainly from the contour of the ribs. Independently, however, of its nature, another difficulty presented itself in the vaulting of the nave, in relation to that of the side aisles; the latter had been vaulted with square compartments; but as the nave was twice the width of the aisles, or nearly so, every two bays were taken to form the square compartment; the immense span, however, of this vault, and the existence of an intermediate pier in each bay serving no purpose, would seem to have suggested the introduction of a supplementary rib across the nave, the web being filled in between this and the diagonal ribs, and this formed what is known as the hexapartite vault (see plan and section, &c., *Plates II. IV. V.* and *VI.*) This vault, however, had two inconveniences: in the first place, the diagonal rib, by its greater projection, hid a portion of one side of the windows; and in the second, the main thrust of the vault was exerted on every alternate pier only. It was true that additional strength could be given to these piers; and the windows, by being brought closer together towards the central rib, would not have had their light interfered with by the diagonal ribs; the former was done at the Abbaye aux Hommes, giving a lopsided appearance to the clerestory openings (see *Plate VI.*); the latter would have placed the windows out of the axis of these in the side aisles, which were naturally in the centre of each square compartment. The next step taken, therefore, appears in the first bay of the nave of the Abbaye aux Dames;[1] and in the transept (*Plates XVI.*[a] and *XVII.*), where, instead of the square hexapartite vault, we have an oblong compartment, whose width is equal to half its length, and with diagonal and transverse ribs only, forming what is called the quadripartite vault.

Up to this epoch the transverse rib of the nave had been circular, the diagonal rib generally an ellipse. This form of arch was not only difficult to erect and to form the centre for, but was essentially weak in construction, requiring very considerable abutment to resist its thrust: besides this, in order that the formerets or wall-ribs (which in these oblong compartments were half the width only of the transverse ribs) should be of

[1] With the exception of this first bay, the nave is vaulted in a peculiar manner, which is neither hexapartite nor quadripartite, the intermediate rib in this case carries an arch, which, rising to the apse of the vault, serves but to support the keystone of the diagonal ribs and the upper ridge of the web.

equal height with the transverse and diagonal ribs, they were obliged to be stilted to so great an extent, that the web between became extremely awkward to construct, and was ungainly in form. These difficulties were all met by the introduction of the pointed arched rib, a stronger form, which exerted less thrust, and accommodated itself at once to all the problems of ribbed vaulting, chiefly from the fact that any number of arches of the same height could be struck from the same springing. It is probably to this introduction of the pointed arch rib that the Gothic style owes its chief impetus. The constructive principle of the pointed arch had long been known; it was used by the Assyrians for their subterranean vaults; it was introduced by the Arabs in their mosques from the ninth century; but its employment in ribbed vaulting dates from the twelfth century—the choir of the abbey of St. Denis (A.D. 1140) being probably the earliest example. After the introduction of the pointed rib, the elliptical arch was abandoned; circular arches were employed for the diagonal ribs, and pointed ones for the transverse and wall ribs. There are cases where even the diagonal ribs are pointed, as in Bayeux Cathedral (*Plates XXVIII. XXIX. XXXIII. XXXIV.*) and the church of St. Ouen (*Plate XL.*), as also where the wall-ribs are stilted; but these form exceptions.

But slight subsequent modifications are to be found in French vaulting; except in the elaboration of the rib mouldings, and in some cases the application of decorative pendants and other ornaments to the ribs, as found in the church of St. Jacques at Dieppe, and in the choir and eastern chapels of St. Pierre at Caen. In England already in the thirteenth century was introduced the ridge rib; and, in later periods, other supplementary ribs, for the best description of which, and the ultimate grouping of them into the fan-vault (a combination entirely confined to England), we would refer the student to Professor G. G. Scott's lectures delivered at the Royal Academy in 1870, and published in the professional journals of that year.

It would scarcely be possible here also, without copious diagrams, to enter into the difference in the formation of the web in English and French vaults. In this country they were formed in courses of stone, of equal depth throughout the course, so that they dipped towards the diagonal ribs, as in the cloisters of Westminster Abbey. In France they were laid horizontal, or nearly so, according to whether the keystones of the transverse or wall ribs were at the same level, or lower than those of the diagonal ribs; besides this difference, the form of the English web was cylindrical, of the French domical. At Bayeux it was as nearly as possible cylindrical, being an exception to the general rule. The domical form of it is shown in the church of St. Ouen (*Plate XL.*)

We have hitherto taken no notice of the means adopted to resist the thrust of the vault. In the Roman period they trusted almost entirely to the thickness of their walls; or, such buttresses as were employed were concealed, as in the Pantheon, or masked under the forms of decorative columns.

In the Abbaye aux Hommes they employed a demicylindrical or half-barrel vault over the triforium gallery, as shown in *Plate V.*; this continuous vault, however, was really not required throughout its whole length, the thrust of the vault being concentrated through the ribs at their springing, or a little above it. In the Abbaye aux Dames, therefore (the next example in point of date in Normandy), we find a simple flying-buttress thrown across above the aisles and at the foot of each rib.[1] In both these cases the aisle roof covered over and hid these constructive forms; and the cathedral of Bayeux shows us the first example in this publication of the flying-buttress as an external feature, and decorated accordingly (*Plates XXVIII. XXIX. XXXI. XXXII.*) In this instance the thrust of the vault is twice transmitted to the outer walls, in consequence of the side and choir chapels. In the church of St. Ouen at Rouen (*Plate XL.*), we see the single flying-buttress, though the elliptical form of its arch is not pleasing.

[1] For reasons given in our description of this church, this flying-buttress was not of sufficient power, nor was it placed high enough, and the vault began to push out the walls, necessitating its destruction, and the insertion of a wooden vault painted in imitation of stone in its place (see *Plate XVI.*)

DESCRIPTION OF THE PLATES,

WITH NOTICES OF

THE BUILDINGS DELINEATED.

CHAPEL OF LA GRANDE MALADRERIE, NEAR CAEN.

PLATE I., Frontispiece.

THE frontispiece to this volume contains the representation of an entrance doorway, and some architectural details, from a church in the village of St. Germain de Blanche-Herbe, commonly called "La Maladrerie," from a lazar-house founded there by Henry II. A.D. 1161. The village is situated about one mile west of Caen, and the ornamental detail of the doorway principally consists of an archivolt richly adorned with a sharp chevron moulding, interspersed with foliage and grotesque heads, each angle of the chevron being filled with a different design. The string-courses placed beneath the doorway consist of two different patterns, as also the corbel-table above. The sunk panels in the angle are taken from another building. [This chapel of La Maladrerie is situated in the village, and must not be confounded with the chapel attached to the ancient lazar-house, which was destroyed in 1826 (after Pugin's visit to it), to make way for the new "Maison centrale de detention."]

In the vicinity of this village, and at a place on the opposite side of the river, are the celebrated *quarries* from which the noted *Caen-stone* is now, and has for many centuries been, obtained. This stone, like that of Bath, in England, is soft, and easily worked; but it is of a more compact substance and of finer grain: its weight is 150 pounds to the French cubic foot in the quarry. The quarries are worked in the manner of caves, and thus guarded against exposure to the weather, to preserve the surface of the rocks from frost. Most of the stone is obtained from a stratum between 20 and 36 feet from the surface. The mode of working the quarries is by excavating chambers of 25 feet, at the extremities of which solid piers are left to support the roof, which is 20 feet in height. The stones are raised through shafts, at the top of which are large wheels, turned by two or three men. The ground landlord usually lets a piece of land, measuring 200 by 100 French feet, on lease for nine years. During the Norman dynasty in England, the Caen-stone was imported into this island in large quantities. It is related that it was employed in London Bridge, the Tower of London, Westminster Abbey, Canterbury Cathedral, &c. Ducarel has quoted some charters showing the estimation in which it was held.

[According to the late Mr. C. W. Smith, the Caen-stone as now quarried and used both in Normandy and England, is much inferior to that which was used in the abbeys and churches of Caen from the eleventh to the fifteenth century. In order to ascertain the exact truth of the matter, Mr. Smith visited Caen, and made a careful examination of the buildings there and in the vicinity, and having obtained an old map of the locality, he found places named in French "The Hollow Way," "The Old Quarry," "The New Quarry," "The Little Quarry," all situated in the immediate vicinity of the great churches and castle of Caen; there were in fact quarries almost underneath the churches, all of which had been deserted for three or four centuries. On going inside them he found stone precisely similar to that of which the old churches were built; and which, though belonging to the same geological series, were very different in point of durability from that Caen-stone of which the modern buildings in London were constructed. In one church, "St. Pierre," the elaborate stone work of the fifteenth century was in an almost perfect state of preservation; no stone, however, at present brought from Caen, would bear anything like that degree of weathering, as it was far from being equally durable with that of bygone times.]

The stones known in France by the name of *Carreaux d'Allemagne* are much used for floors of rooms in Normandy, and nearly all over the kingdom. Great quantities are also exported. A fossil crocodile was found in these quarries in 1817, perfect in form, with the scales clearly defined. It consequently excited much curiosity amongst geologists.

ABBEY CHURCH OF ST. STEPHEN, L'ABBAYE AUX HOMMES, CAEN.

PLATES II.—XII.

The church belonging to this abbey is stated by Huet[1] to have been built by William, Duke of Normandy, in 1064; but the Abbé de la Rue argues, from the phraseology of the foundation charter, that the edifice was not commenced till after the conquest of England, in 1066.[2] Lanfranc, afterwards Archbishop of Canterbury, was appointed the first abbot, and he began the building of the church;[3] which was completed under his successor, William de Bonne Ame; and, according to the testimony of Ordericus Vitalis, a contemporary historian, it was dedicated in 1077.[4] Some writers have indeed referred this event to the year 1073, while others date the dedication of the church in 1081 or 1086;[5] but the precise and circumstantial narrative of Ordericus gives superior probability to the date which he has advanced, and which De la Rue has adopted.

[Mr. Parker remarks:[6]—"It is rather singular that, notwithstanding

[1] Huet, *Origines de Caen*, 2d edit. 1706, p. 175.

[2] *Essais Historiques sur la Ville de Caen*, tom. ii. p. 52. In the foundation charter William takes the title of "Rex Anglorum," and bestows on the monastery much English property; in reference to the building of the abbey he says, *disposui construendum;* words which imply that the work was not executed when the charter was granted. See *Neustria Pia*, p. 626.

[3] In the chartulary of St. Stephen, among several contracts entered into by Lanfranc, while abbot, is one relating to four acres of land whence stone was procured to build the monastery ("*unde lapides extrahuntur ad opus monasterii*"). Huet asserts that the stone used for this edifice was brought from the quarries of Vaucelles and Allemagne, near Caen: which statement is objected to by De la Rue, who, however, does not mention the place whence the stone was obtained.—*Orig. de Caen*, p. 179; *Essais Historiques*, tome ii. p. 59.

[4] *Orderici Hist. Eccles.* lib. v. ad ann. 1077. [5] Huet, *Orig. de Caen*, p. 175; and *Dumoustier*, p. 625.

[6] Paper read before the Royal Institute of British Architects, Jan. 26th, 1863, and published in their *Transactions* 1862-63.]

the notoriety of those foundations, it is difficult to ascertain the exact year in which the buildings were commenced; the authorities differ considerably in the dates, both of foundation and of consecration: 1064, 1066, and 1070 are mentioned for the foundation; and 1071, 1073, 1077, and 1078 for the dedication of St. Stephen's. Lanfranc was sent to Rome in 1059 to make peace with the pope, Nicholas II., and returned in 1060 with the pardon and its conditions agreed upon: the foundation, therefore, could not have been before that year, and as Lanfranc was made abbot of St. Stephen's in 1066, it is probable that some of the buildings were then ready, although the consecration of the church did not take place until eleven years afterwards, in 1077. Trinity Church (Abbaye aux Dames) is said to have been consecrated in 1066. Possibly it was not convenient to carry on these two large works at the same time, and Matilda's church may have been finished before William's was commenced; or what is more probable is that either a temporary wooden church was the one consecrated in 1066, or that only just as much as was necessary for performing the service was then ready, and the altar was consecrated—the papal bull of foundation, granting special privileges to the abbey of St. Stephen, is dated in 1068. The abbey was richly endowed with lands both in Normandy and England. Lanfranc was made Archbishop of Canterbury in 1070, leaving the buildings of his abbey very incomplete, to be carried on by his successors."

As will be seen on referring to *Plate II*., the plan of the church consists of—a vestibule at the west end, to which entrance is obtained through three doorways—a nave of eight bays with side aisles—a chapel of three bays at the north-west end—a transept of five bays (two of which have each at the north and south extremities respectively a chapel with an intermediate vault of two bays at the level of the aisle vault)—a small apse on the eastern side of the southern chapel, and a third bay to the northern chapel—a choir of four bays and the apse with side aisles round, and a series of thirteen chapels, seven of which form the chevet. This choir and chevet, dating from the thirteenth century, replaced the original choir of the eleventh century, which consisted, according to

Mr. Fergusson[1] (and taken by him from Ramée, *Histoire Générale de l'Architecture*), of two apses at the north and south ends of the transept, and a central choir of two bays and the apse, the side aisles being continued to the north and south of the two bays, and terminating by a straight wall. No authority is given for this termination, and as in Romsey abbey church, where a similar arrangement occurs, internally the aisle terminates with an apse, this may possibly have been the case in the original choir of the Abbaye aux Hommes.

[2]The earliest parts of the abbey church now remaining are—the east wall of the central tower—the outer walls of the transepts and nave—and the original west front, which forms the back of the present western towers. These parts were probably built between 1073, when the original choir was finished, and the conclusion of the reign of William I., in 1087; and they do, in fact, comprise the main structure of the present nave and transepts, but so much disguised and altered in appearance by the insertion of the vault that considerable care is required to distinguish the original parts. The west front was long considered as the especial type of the Norman style at the time of the Conquest; it now appears from the close examination of M. Bouet, that it cannot possibly belong to that period, but is the work of the next generation, when the art of building had considerably improved and the masons had become more skilful. The upper portion of the towers belongs to the latter part of the eleventh century, the spires are of the thirteenth, being amongst the earliest Gothic spires. The vaults of the nave transept date from the twelfth century, great changes having then been made in the arrangement of the clerestory, to which we shall allude farther on. Mr. Parker remarks: "There is no direct historical evidence of the period at which the central vault was constructed, but large benefactions to the abbey are recorded in the time of Henry II. about 1160-1165, and the architectural character of the details of the vault agrees perfectly with other buildings of that period."

The exact date of the reconstruction of the choir is not known. It has been erroneously attributed to the middle of the fourteenth century.

[1] Fergusson's *History of Architecture*.]
[2] The principal dates and facts here are taken from Mr. Parker's paper already referred to.]

during the administration of Simon de Trevieres; this, however, would be much too late a date for it, and M. Bouet has shown that the traditions setting it down as his work refer probably to the construction of the Chapelle Halbout (called morning chapel on *Plate II.*), which was sometimes used as a choir during alterations in the actual choir. Mr. Parker assigns 1230 to 1250 as the probable period, though the character of the detail is such that it might safely be ascribed to the beginning of the thirteenth or even the end of the twelfth century.

The central tower or lantern fell down in 1566, leaving the eastern wall only standing; the western side was rebuilt in 1602, and the two eastern piers of the nave along with it. At the same period, or during the next twenty years, were reconstructed, according to M. Bouet,[1] the vault of the nave tribune, originally built at the same time as the nave vault, the vaulting of the side aisles, and the pierced balustrade of the tribune.

In the seventeenth century also were rebuilt the northern side of the clerestory and tribune of the choir, the southern side of the latter, together with the vaulting, and some of the vaulting also of the choir aisle on the north side. In the eighteenth century the upper portions of the south-west spire, injured by lightning, were rebuilt; and in the commencement of this century much restoration throughout, including, unfortunately, a general scraping of the wall surfaces, rendering it very difficult to distinguish the older parts from the new.

Returning now to a description of the building in detail, the western front exhibits different characters according to the period of its erection. The lower portion, built towards the close of the eleventh century, and added to the original west façade, is extremely plain, the decoration being confined to the archivolts of the doorways, which consist of two orders and a label moulding.]

Above these entrances is a double range of semicircular windows. The central compartment, corresponding to the nave in width, is finished by a high pointed gable, and the two lateral ones are carried up into lofty towers, supporting octagonal spires. The towers consist of three

[1 *Analyse Architecturale de l'Abbaye de St. Etienne de Caen*, by G. Bouet, p. 134.]

stories, the lowest of which, on each face, has a range of seven blank arcades, without any mouldings or imposts; the second has five arches of a larger size, two of which are pierced, and have shafts, capitals, and bases. The third and uppermost story exhibits two large arches, rising from clustered shafts, and inclosing smaller arches, which are also pierced with windows. The towers are finished by a cornice, above which rise sixteen rich perforated pinnacles, surrounding the base of the spire, the form and tracery of the pinnacles being different on each tower. The north-east angle of the northern tower is flanked by a semicircular buttress, or staircase-turret, partaking throughout of the characteristics of the square faces of the tower. [The spire itself has angle rolls, and is decorated with bands of five courses of stone cut in imitation of shingles, three plain courses of stone intervening between each band.

The external wall of the side aisles and triforium gallery is strengthened by flat buttresses, the relieving arch between, however, being pointed and not circular, as shown in the drawing (*Plate V.*). The lower portion of this wall is now masked by the classic corridor of the Lycée or school attached to the abbey church. The exterior of the clerestory of the nave is decorated with a continuous arcade, consisting of twenty-two arches. eight of which are pierced with windows.]

At the extremity of the north transept are three very shallow buttresses, which rise from the ground to the sills of the clerestory windows. unbroken by any interruption, but here they meet with a string-course, above which the two outer ones are continued to the summit of the ends of the gable, while the centre one is reduced in depth. Over this latter buttress is a window; and between the buttresses are six other windows, arranged in double rows. Eastward of the transepts is a series of blank arches, remarkable for their mouldings, which consist of a flat, wide, and very shallow band; and here the mixture of the pointed with the Norman or circular architecture commences.[1]

[The external decoration of the choir will be best understood by reference to *Plates IX. X.* and *XI.*, the only part not shown being the elevation of the chevet chapels, these on plan form a series of convex

[1] Cotman's *Architectural Antiquities of Normandy*, vol. i. p. 23.

curves with buttresses in the angles of their junction; from these buttresses to the centre of each chapel wall arches are thrown across to carry the cornice and parapet,[1] which becomes one large semicircle on plan; a somewhat similar arrangement is to be found in the choirs of Bayeux and Coutances cathedrals.

Returning now to the nave (the interior of which is represented in *Plates IV, V, and VI.*) we find it to be divided into eight bays, each bay being divided vertically into three stories. The lower one has semicircular arches of two orders and stilted, carried on attached columns and piers, and opening to the side aisles. The middle story has similar arches not stilted, on columns of less height, and opening to the triforium gallery; and the upper story, or clerestory, has lofty and narrow arches decorated with the embattled fret ornament, with windows behind, and sub- or smaller arches on the side of the intermediate rib only.

The side aisles M. Bouet has shown were originally covered with half-barrel vaults intersected and without ribs. In the seventeenth century a new vault was constructed with pointed ribs, thus raising the floor of the triforium gallery and hiding the bases of the columns and piers there. The balustrade pierced with quatrefoils belongs also to this period. The half-barrel vault of the triforium, reconstructed in the seventeenth century, was copied from that which was erected probably at the same time as the nave vaults, and served as an abutment for them; the original covering being a wooden roof.[2]

Previous to the investigations of Mr. J. H. Parker, M. Ruprich Robert, and M. Bouet, it had been supposed that the existing clerestory wall, with its openings, was of the same date as the lower walls of the nave. The discovery, however, of two arches above the web of the present vault by Mr. Ruprich Robert, in 1860, pointed out that, with the arches in front of the windows, there were in each double bay of the nave a series of four arches carried on columns. It had also been assumed that the

[[1] See drawing in *Institute Transactions*, Jan. 26, 1863, attached to Mr. Parker's paper, and taken from the *Monasticon Gallicanum*, 1684; on this drawing will also be seen the central tower, the upper portion of which was rebuilt in the seventeenth century, as well as four other towers containing the stairs which lead to the roof. [2] Bouet, *Analyse Architecturale*, p. 221.]

nave and transepts were vaulted in the first instance, whereas now it is generally agreed that the first church (as all churches in the north of France at this epoch) was covered with a wooden roof. The exact nature of this wooden roof and its relation to the four arched openings, and to the vaulting shafts, has been the subject of much conjecture. These vaulting shafts (see plan *Plates II.* and *V.*) consist alternately of a three-quarter detached column with and without a pilaster; they are both of the same date as the nave walls, and one of the points in dispute turns upon the original object in the difference of their form.

Mr. Parker believes that the shaft with pilaster was made more important in order to carry an arch spanning the nave, as in the abbey church of Cerisy, near Bayeux, thus serving the purpose of a truss, the intermediate shaft carrying a secondary truss: he does not explain, however, how this intermediate shaft was coupled to the central column of the four arcades above-mentioned.

M. Ruprich Robert points out that the absence of any external buttresses to the clerestory of Abbaye aux Hommes is a sufficient reason that there should be no arch inside, and that the buttresses of Cerisy, its later date than that supposed, and other differences in the arrangement of the arcades, preclude the possibility of its being taken as a precedent for the Abbaye aux Hommes. He believes that the difference in the vaulting shafts is due to the fact of its having been originally intended to have a principal and secondary trusses only and no arch, and assumes that the two central arcades were the result of an after-thought, there being only two projected at first, viz. those in front of the windows.

M. Bouet, we believe, originated Mr. Parker's opinion as regards the arch spanning the nave; he seems, however, in his *Analyse Architecturale* (p. 35), to entertain the idea that it was intended from the beginning to vault over the nave with quadripartite vaults, taking in two bays each, and he points out in support of this theory the means taken to counterbalance the thrust of this nave vault by the conjunction of the inner and outer wall of the clerestory with solid masonry on each side of the main ribs. and the isolation of the four arcades in the centre of each double bay. whilst at Cerisy the arcade fills up the whole width. This, however, does not explain the use of the intermediate shaft. Between these various opinions it is difficult to draw any line; we believe, however, on the whole, that M. Ruprich Robert is right, and that Mr. Parker's suggestion of the arch is not tenable. This becomes the more evident when we examine the elevations of the original clerestory walls as restored in M. Bouet's and M. Ruprich Robert's works, for in both of them the pilaster and shaft are carried up to the level of the springing of the four arcades, far above, therefore, any possible springing of an arch spanning the nave. Mr. Parker himself allows "that the difference in the size and form of the alternate piers is, taken by itself, no positive proof that there were original transverse arches of stone to carry the roof, as at Cerisy; the same arrangement occurs at Winchester and at Waltham, which were not vaulted, and had no transverse arches; so that they must have been used for carrying the principal timbers only;" on the other hand, the strength of the original walls behind the transverse ribs of the present vault would be an argument in favour of the transverse arch were it not for the continuation of this shaft above-mentioned.

The Halbout chapel at the north-west end of the church, built in the commencement of the fourteenth century, was in great part destroyed by the Protestants, and "the present tracery of the windows," M. Bouet remarks, "may date from 1620, though portions have been restored in this century."

At the northern and southern extremities of the transept are small chapels of two bays each vaulted at the level of the aisle vault; this was a common feature both in Normandy and England at this period (eleventh century). These chapels were terminated on the eastern side by small apses, one of which probably forms the foundation of the present apse (now used as a sacristy) on the south side; the other apse has been replaced by what we may regard as a third bay to the chapel.

The first of these two, as will be seen from the drawings (*Plates VII. and VIII.*), is an extremely beautiful example of early thirteenth century work. The lower portion of the chapel may be looked upon as a dado or base, on which are placed the columns and coupled shafts carrying the vault; these columns and shafts are detached from the wall, leaving a narrow corridor behind at a height of 9 ft. 6 in. from the floor, thus giving a light and elegant appearance to the chapel.

It is singular that notwithstanding the immense importance of the choir of the Abbaye aux Hommes, there should be no record of its date. Previous to the investigations of M. Bouet and Mr. Parker it had usually been assigned to the fourteenth century, being attributed, as before stated, to Abbot Simon, 1314-1344.[1] M. Hippeau, however, has shown[2] that in the epitaph of the Abbot Simon there is no mention of the choir, which would certainly have been made if it had been executed during his abbacy; and M. Bouet points out that the form of letter on the tomb of the architect of the choir accords so far with the style of work as to bring back the date to the commencement of the thirteenth century, or even the last years of the twelfth. "In fact," he says, "although at first sight the choir appears to be entirely Gothic, there still remain a sufficient number of details purely Norman in their style to render this last date admissible. For instance, the zigzags in the choir-arches and in the wall-ribs of the choir recall to mind those in the cathedral of Canterbury, in those portions built about 1178 by William of Sens.[3]

Referring to the similarity between these two buildings, Prof. Willis, in his work on the latter, remarks: "Now Lanfranc, before he was made Archbishop of Canterbury, was the first abbot of the monastery of St. Stephen at Caen, the church of which was built under his direction, being begun in 1064, and dedicated in 1077, after his appointment to Canterbury. The two churches were therefore building at the same time. The church at Caen, like that at Canterbury, has its original choir replaced by one in the thirteenth century, probably for a similar reason—enlargement. The portions which it retains are alike in plan and arrangement to the corresponding parts of Canterbury, alike in the number of piers, in having western towers, transepts without aisles, a central tower, eastern chapels to the transepts, and the pillar and vault at the end of each transept. In some of the churches erected in England by the

[[1] Mr. Britton, however, in his first edition, protests against this date, judging from the style of architecture alone.]
[[2] *Monographie de l'Abbaye de St. Etienne*, p. 310.   [3] *Analyse Architecturale*, Bouet, p. 70.]

Bishop of Durham, Hugues de Pinsit (*vulgo* Pudsey), we find capitals decorated with leaves, terminated by small volutes;[1] similar leaves to these are found in the frieze and capitals of the choir of St. Stephen (*Plates IX. XII.*). In another church (Sherburn Chapel, 1183), built by the same prelate, is a capital very similar to one in the Abbaye aux Hommes. It is therefore natural to suppose that these edifices belong to about the same period."

On the other hand, M. Hippeau (p. 340)[2] remarks "that in 1250 the abbey was in debt to the fourth part of its revenue; may we not, therefore," says he, speaking of these debts, "attribute them with certainty to the expenses caused by the construction of the choir?"

Mr. Parker,[3] in endeavouring to fix the date, compares the work in the choir of St. Stephen with that of the cathedral of Lisieux, and comes to the conclusion that "the style of the choir and apse of St. Stephen's at Caen evidently comes between the nave and the apse of Lisieux, the latter being pure Norman Gothic, and in the opinion of the best Norman antiquaries the date cannot be put before 1200, and between that and 1220 is the probable date. The only vestige of the Romanesque style is the use of the zigzag ornament in the moulding of the arches of the choir, and, perhaps, the very singular use of plain segmental arches to carry the vault of the triforium gallery, partly enriched by the ornamental heads of the arches of the arcade in front of them. This is a clumsy piece of construction, which would hardly have been used after the Gothic style was established."

The new choir was erected in consequence of the demand for a much greater space than had hitherto been required for the church services. The number of reliques also brought from the East at the epoch of the Crusades called for the erection of numerous chapels, and the choir-aisle to give access to them.

The new choir proper consisted of four bays and the apse, the side aisles were continued round the latter, and a series of thirteen chapels, seven of which formed the chevet, were added. The division walls

[1 See Plate in M. Bonet's work, p. 72. (Tynemouth.)]
[2 *Monographie de l'Abbaye de St. Etienne.* 3 *Paper in Transactions.* R. I. B. A., 1865–66.]

between these chevet chapels were carried to a height of only six feet, so that, as it were, a double colonnade was formed (*see plan*), producing a very beautiful effect. The extreme lightness and elegance of this part of the church, the variety in the perspective, and the play of light and shade, constitute in this chevet one of the finest specimens of early French architecture in Normandy.

Reference to the drawings (*Plates IX. X. XI.*) will show the nature of the interior of this new choir. The main heights of the nave are carried through. The arches of the seven bays of the apse are stilted to bring them to the same height as those in the choir; a similar arrangement is found at Canterbury, in contradistinction to the lancet-arches of the apses of most of our cathedrals. The coupled columns of the apse are similar to those of Canterbury. The arches, however, of the triforium gallery are far lighter and more elegant in the Abbaye aux Hommes. In the choir these arches are semicircular, inclosing two pointed arches; in the apse they are pointed. In the clerestory there are two windows to each bay of the choir, one to each of the apse. In front of the former is a central pointed and two half arches carried on slender columns, there being a narrow corridor behind them.

It is only of late years that the subsequent history of this choir has been thoroughly investigated; and M. Bouet has shown in his analysis of the present structure that a considerable portion was rebuilt in the seventeenth century.

This reconstruction was necessitated by the ravages caused by the Protestants, for, at the beginning of the seventeenth century, the whole church was a perfect wreck compared with its present condition. The choir, in fact, was in so bad a state that its rebuilding was deemed hopeless, and permission had been given to make use of its old materials in the restoration of the nave and other parts of the church. Fortunately, however, this was not done; and so much care was taken in the reconstruction as to render it a difficult task to distinguish between the old work and the new.

The investigations of M. Bouet have shown that the nave-vault, the half-barrel vault over the triforium gallery, the balustrades to the same, the side-aisle vault, the greater portion of the roofs, a portion of the Halbout chapel before referred to, the two great piers of the central tower adjoining the nave, the northern side of the clerestory and triforium gallery of the choir, the southern side of the latter, together with the vaulting, and some of the vaulting of the choir-aisle on the north side, were restored, if not rebuilt, in the first quarter of the seventeenth century; many changes being afterwards made in the roofs.

In the commencement of the eighteenth century the western front and towers were restored, and the choir and chapels were enclosed with magnificent "grilles," all of these latter having been destroyed at the time of the Revolution. The establishment of the Lycée or "departemental" school in Caen at the beginning of this century called for the destruction of many of the old abbey buildings, which is much to be regretted; at the same time, however, since thirty years, the church has been intrusted to the care of intelligent architects, M. Guy and M. Ruprich Robert, under whose hands the present fabric bids fair to be properly preserved and cared for.]

CHURCH OF THE HOLY TRINITY, L'ABBAYE AUX DAMES, CAEN.

PLATES XIII.—XVII.

If the testimonies of Ordericus Vitalis and William of Junieges are to be implicitly credited, this church must have been commenced, if not far advanced, before the year 1064;[1] and it is said to have been dedicated in June, 1066, by Maurilius, Archbishop of Rouen. With the annexed abbey, it was endowed with ample revenues by Matilda, wife of Duke William, who, about the same time, founded and established the neighbouring monastery of St. Stephen, for monks. The royal pair had married in contravention of a canon of the church, which prohibits

[1] These historians state that the first abbess, Matilda, died in 1112, after governing the abbey more than forty-seven years. —See Huet, Origines de Caen, p. 177.

marriages between persons of certain degrees of kindred.¹ That of the Trinity was founded for nuns of the Benedictine order, and was invested with extensive manorial rights, privileges, and immunities.² Its annual revenue was estimated at 70,000 livres. The abbesses were of distinguished rank and of high connection. Among them we find the names of Bourbon, Valois, Albret, Montmorency, and Cécily, the youngest daughter of the founder, who, it is related, was devoted by her parents to the monastic life on the day of dedicating the church. The nuns of this house were mostly of noble birth, and were invested with many privileges and exemptions. They were not bound by vows, were allowed to see their friends in private apartments, had the charge of younger relatives, and were permitted to eat meat at their meals on days when fasting was enjoined in other houses.

[Researches made at intervals since the year 1850 show that with the exception of the crypt, scarcely any portion of the first church founded in 1064 remains. M. Ruprich Robert, however, the architect employed by the French government to superintend the restoration, has made the most careful examination of the building, and has published a pamphlet³

¹ William, Duke of Normandy, commonly and inaccurately called the Conqueror, married his first cousin, Matilda, daughter of Baldwin, Count of Flanders. This offended the clergy, and particularly Lanfranc, then resident at Bec, who ventured to reprehend the duke in rather harsh terms. Indignant at his clerical insolence, the duke banished the "proud priest." An interview again occurred, and Lanfranc engaged to visit the supreme pontiff, who granted a dispensation to the duke and his duchess on their founding two abbeys, respectively for nuns and monks. [Mr. Parker, in his paper before quoted, draws attention to a communication made by the late Mr. Stapleton to the *Archæological Journal*, vol. iii., in which he endeavours to show that there was another cause for this besides consanguinity—that Matilda had previously been married to Gerbodo, the *avoué* of St. Bertin, and that the issue of this marriage were Gerbodo, Earl of Chester, Frederick, and Gundrada, wife of William Warren and foundress of Lewes Priory. He endeavours to show that the cause of their excommunication was that the Pope had refused to consent to her divorce from her first husband, and consequently that her marriage with William would have been null, if they had not succeeded in making their peace with the Pope.]

² By the Domesday Survey it appears that it possessed many estates in the counties of Essex, Dorset, Devon, and Gloucester, in England. These distant lands were occasionally visited by the lady abbess. M. de la Rue tells us that he saw a diary of the Abbess Georgetta du Molley Bacon, in which it is recorded that she embarked at the Fort of Caen, Aug. 16, 1370, with fifteen attendants, and landed at London, whence she proceeded to Felsted, in Essex; and that she returned home the following year.—*Essais Historiques*, &c., tom. ii. p. 19.

[³ *L'Eglise St. Trinité* (Abbaye aux Dames) *et l'Eglise St. Etienne* (Abbaye aux Hommes) à *Caen*. Caen, 1864, 8vo.]

on the abbey church, from which we are able to glean the following particulars.

The nave is composed of two rows of piers, and two walls forming the side aisles. The line of these walls is not parallel to that of the piers: that on the north side inclining inwards as it approaches the transept; that on the south side slightly outwards. It would seem therefore as if a more ancient nave had existed, and that in its reconstruction the central axis had been deviated from its original line. The arches also of the nave are carried only on single shafts, except at the transept and the western tower ends, where they rest on two shafts side by side (see *Plate XVI^a*.), a disposition which seems to belong to another design. The side-aisle walls are pierced with circular headed windows, the axes of which do not correspond with the side-aisle vaulting; and flat buttresses now destroyed (though restored in plan, *Plate XVI^a*., from M. Ruprich Robert's woodcut) were placed pretty regularly between these windows. These buttresses therefore were not situated in line with or opposite to the nave-piers. We may therefore conclude that the nave-piers were not built at the same time as the side-aisle walls, but are of later date. These facts and the difference in the style of the capitals and bases of the crypt, the lower part of the towers, and of the nave-piers, have led M. Ruprich Robert to place in the following chronological order those parts of the church which are Norman in style.

To the first period belong the crypt, the central tower up to the roof of the church, the lower portion of the western towers and front, the walls of the transept, and the side-aisle walls of the nave.

To the second period: the piers of the nave, the vaults of the side aisle, the upper portion of the towers, a part of the transept walls (triforium), and the choir.

To the third period: the walls of the nave above the nave-arches, the vaulting shafts and clerestory of the transept, and the vaulting of the nave and transepts, with the flying-buttresses under the aisle roof.

The work of the first period M. Robert assigns as that of Matilda, as well as four apses, two on either side of the choir; two of these to the north, shown on plan, have been rebuilt on the old foundations; the remains of the two others on the south side have been discovered under the thirteenth century chapel (salle capitulaire).

Possibly from the difficulty of carrying on two such large works as the Abbaye aux Hommes and the Abbaye aux Dames at the same time, the continuation of the latter may have been deferred till the end of the eleventh century, the date of the second period. Considerable changes were then made, as already pointed out, in the position of the nave-piers. The choir was also built at this period. Its plan does not accord with the ancient crypt, the axes of the windows do not correspond, and the walls are built within those of the crypt. The vault of the choir is groined, without ribs, and belongs to the same epoch as that of the side aisles.

When in the middle of the twelfth century (the third period) it was determined to vault both nave and transept, great additions and alterations were made in the existing structure. In the transept a new clerestory wall was built, and vaulting shafts were added. In the nave the whole of the wall above the arches was rebuilt, including triforium and clerestory; simple shafts to carry the trusses of the original wooden roof had existed, to these were added and carried on corbels small vaulting shafts to receive the diagonal ribs of the vault. The upper order of the nave-arches was added, and decorated with the embattled fret ornament similar to that round the clerestory windows of the Abbaye aux Hommes. The triforium gallery which runs beneath the clerestory windows necessitated an increased thickness of the nave-wall, which was obtained by throwing arches[1] across between the piers. In order to resist the thrust of the new vault flying-buttresses were built across the aisles; as however these buttresses were placed too low, and no buttresses were added to the old aisle walls, the vault began to push out the nave-walls, rendering necessary the destruction of the stone vault and its replacement by a vault in wood and plaster,[2] painted to represent stone.

[1] We have added to Pugin's plate (XVII.) the flying-buttress and supporting arch here mentioned, taking them from M. Ruprich Robert's pamphlet. The vault of the side aisles is a circular barrel-vault, and not pointed as shown in the illustration.]

[2] This wooden and plaster vault is shown in Pugin's drawing (Plate XVI.) Since 1859 it has been replaced by a vault in hollow brick and light stone ribs, and new buttresses have been added to the aisle walls.]

The towers of the west façade were in the twelfth century surmounted by stone spires; these were destroyed in 1360 when the abbey was fortified.

In the thirteenth century the central tower, which had been partially destroyed, was restored, and the story with three pointed-arch windows on each face was added. At the same time was built the chapel on the south side of the choir, which served as the chapter-house. On the north side another chapel was constructed; this was destroyed probably when the hospital buildings were erected under Louis XIV.

Returning now to a description of the plates, the first (*Plate XIII.*) represents the entrance-gateway to the abbey. This has now been destroyed to make way for the new street leading direct up to the hospital gates. It was placed to the south-west of the abbey church, at about 50 yards distance from it.

The crypt, the oldest portion of the abbey church, is shown in *Plate XIV.*; the vaulting is groined, without ribs, and is carried on sixteen columns and eighteen semi-detached shafts: the capitals, two of which are drawn to a larger scale in *Plate XV.*, show clearly their classic origin in the volutes and rows of leaves above the necking.

The plan, *Plate XVI*ª., which has been added to this edition, will serve to explain the peculiar nature of the vaulting of this church. The vestibule, or narthex, is vaulted over by a hexapartite vault; the first bay of the nave with an oblong quadripartite vault; and the eight succeeding bays with four quadripartite vaults, and an intersecting rib and arch. We have already, in our Introductory Essay on Vaulting, drawn attention to the peculiarity of this latter feature, which serves only to carry out the division of the double bay of the nave without materially assisting to carry the vault. It is difficult to understand why, when in the Abbaye aux Hommes the use of such an intermediate rib had been found out, viz. to divide and assist in carrying legitimately

[ª The terms north, south, east, and west have been hitherto adopted to indicate the relative positions of the various parts of the church. The principal axis, however, does not run from west to east, as is usual, but inclines towards the south. The same disposition is found in three other churches of Caen, viz. St. Pierre, St. Gilles, and St. Sauveur.]

the web, it should have been neglected here; and we were inclined to believe that this was the first attempt at the subdivision of the double quadripartite bay. M. Ruprich Robert, however, judging from the more careful workmanship of the ribs, and the introduction of a flying-buttress only at the position required to resist thrust, places the construction of this vault after that of the Abbaye aux Hommes, where, it will be remembered, the thrust is overcome by a continuous half-barrel vault. The main difference in the two examples is found in the formation of the web. The intermediate rib in the Abbaye aux Dames carries a vertical wall, which, rising to the apex of the vault, serves only to support the keystones of the web (which is quadripartite in principle); in the Abbaye aux Hommes the web is formed between the diagonal and intermediate ribs, or, in other terms, forms a conical vault between them (see *Plates XVI. and IV.*)

The centre bay of the transept is a square quadripartite vault; the northern and southern bays have additional ribs carried on vaulting shafts in the centre of the north and south walls of the transept respectively.

The choir consists of two square bays, and the apsidal end with heavy transverse but no diagonal ribs; the triforium is not carried into the choir, there being no aisles. In the apse are two stories with five arcades each, the arches being carried on detached columns with richly carved capitals (*Plate XVI.*); it is vaulted with a semi-dome; and in the centre of the choir is the tomb of the foundress. The erection of the south chapel with three pointed arch openings necessitated the cutting away of the vaulting shafts of the transept, which are now carried above the central arch on corbels. This chapel is a good specimen of thirteenth century work; the vaulting is carried on two piers, with eight attached columns or shafts to each.

The two apses on the north side were rebuilt by M. Ruprich Robert on the old foundations, and, under the chapel above mentioned have been found the traces of two similar apses on the south side, determining the original plan of the east end of the church. M. Robert believes that these four apses and the crypt only were built in Matilda's time, and that no central choir and apse was erected till the end of the eleventh century.

Externally the west front is flanked by two towers; entrance to the church is obtained through three doorways; the two under the towers have circular headed arches of one order, and a tympanum decorated with diaper; the central doorway has circular headed arches of three orders: and the tympanum is decorated with sculpture and supported by a central pier. Over this doorway is an arcade of three arches pierced with windows; and above an arcade of four arches, the two centre ones only carried on columns and pierced, the two side ones being decorative only with the tympanum decorated with diaper. The gable above this has a single circular headed opening, and its whole surface is decorated with diaper. The stories of the towers do not correspond with those in the central bay of the façade, being loftier; over the doorway in each case is a small circular headed window, above on each face three blank arcades carried on coupled columns; over this and above the level of the nave-roof the tower is decorated on each face with an arcade of six arches carried on columns, windows being pierced in two of them only. The upper portions of these towers were destroyed, as has already been noted, in the thirteenth century. At present they are surmounted by a Renaissance balustrade and corbels. It is purposed (1872) to restore this part of the tower, to add an additional story with two circular headed windows, and spires in the style of the thirteenth century. At the south-east end of the south tower is a circular staircase, which now rises to the height it is intended to carry the towers—this also will have a conical spire.

The side-aisle walls are extremely simple, they have the original circular headed windows I have spoken of; new buttresses have been added to assist in the support of the nave-vault, whose thrust is transmitted across the aisles by flying-buttresses; the clerestory (*Plate XVII.*) has flat buttresses, a corbel table, and in each division, corresponding with the bays of the nave, a large window with semicircular arches of two orders, and blank sub-arches on each side. The Norman work of the central tower shows itself in the arcade carried round and partially cut into by the nave-roof; above is the thirteenth century story before alluded to, the whole being crowned by a fifteenth century balustrade, and an octagonal slate roof. It is proposed to remove this balustrade and erect a loftier slate roof with corresponding corner pinnacles. Very little of the transept is visible in consequence of the modern abbey buildings, but the arcading of the nave clerestory is carried round. The apse has similar arcading in two stories corresponding to the interior, with windows in each bay: all this part is inclosed in the abbey buildings.

The following is a summary of the restoration carried out since 1857, under M. Ruprich Robert:—

Entire reconstruction (copied from the old work) of the western façade between the two towers.

The aisle-walls have had new buttresses and corbel-tables with cornice added.

The nave-piers have been rebuilt up to the capitals of the nave-arches, the vaults of the nave have been reconstructed with light stone ribs and hollow brick webs.

In the south transept the insertions under Louis XIV. have been removed, and the original features, such as windows and vaulting shafts, string-courses, &c., established in their place. The mullions of the windows of the Gothic chapel are new.

In the south transept all the decorative features had been destroyed; these have all been restored, and the two apsidal chapels rebuilt. A restored view of the abbey is given in M. Ruprich Robert's work, to which the reader is referred for further information.]

CHURCH OF ST. NICHOLAS, CAEN.

PLATES XVIII. AND XIX.

This edifice is situated in the district of Bourg-l'abbé, so called from belonging to the abbey of St. Stephen, in the same town. [It is commonly cited as a dated example, built in 1083, but Mr. Parker has shown¹ "that this date, like many others, must be received with caution, and requires explanation. The only historical evidence for it is that of a charter in which Duke William grants to the abbey of St. Stephen a certain piece of waste land outside the walls of Caen, and near to that abbey. This district was then formed into a parish, and the church of St. Nicholas built by the monks of St. Stephen's upon it. All that the historical evidence proves, therefore, is that no part of the church can be earlier than that date; but how long it was building, or when it was consecrated, we have no evidence. The district granted was so extensive that within it were already two small parishes with churches, which had previously been given to the abbey of the Holy Trinity. This led to a lawsuit, in which it was ultimately decided that the parishes belonging to the nuns were confined to the houses built previous to the grant, but all the rest belonged to the monks. In after times this led to much confusion when the houses were rebuilt and new ones erected, but it proves that there was no parish of St. Nicholas before that time, or the boundaries of it would have been known. The early capitals in the church of St. Nicholas are of the same character as those in St. Stephen's of the second period, as in the western towers the resemblance is so close that they may reasonably be supposed to be the work of the same hands, and they are excellent examples of that rude Ionic before mentioned as one of the characteristic features of the last quarter of the eleventh century."]

The general form of this church is that of the Latin cross, divided into a nave and choir, and having, at the intersection of these with the transept, a low tower, surmounted by a gabled roof. The most remarkable part of the edifice is the semi-circular apse which terminates the choir, resembling that of the church of the Holy Trinity, but covered by a conical roof, rising higher than the other parts of the church. Mr. Turner says, "The height of this roof is so much greater than in the choir, as almost to justify the suspicion that it was no part of the original plan, but was an addition of a subsequent, though certainly not of a remote, era. Were the line of it continued to the central tower, it would wholly

[¹ In a paper read before the Royal Institute of British Architects, before referred to.]

block up and conceal the windows there. The discrepancy observable in the style of its architecture may also possibly be regarded as enforcing the same opinion."[1]

[Mr. Fergusson (*Hist. Arch.*) remarks: "It is the only church so far as I know in Normandy that retains the original external covering of its apse. This consists of a high pyramidal roof of stone, following to the eastward the polygonal form of the apse, and extending one bay towards the west" (as shown in *Plate XIX.* of this book). "From an examination of the central tower it is clear that this was not the original pitch of the church roof, which was nearly as low in all Norman churches as in those of Auvergne. In this instance the roof over the apse was a sort of semi-spire placed over an altar to mark externally the importance of the portion of the church beneath it." M. de Caumont also writes that "having examined the church, he noticed on the gable which terminates the nave the traces of the old roof, which was much less elevated than the present conical termination; and this observation applies equally to the stone covering of the apsidal chapels on the east elevation of the two transepts."

The upper portion of the western tower, which is corbelled out and has a saddle-back roof, is an addition of the fifteenth century.] The engravings (*Plates XVIII.* and *XIX.*) represent a *ground plan* of the semi-circular or apsidal end of the church; also an elevation of part of the exterior of the same, two sections, and capitals and bases.

CHURCH OF THAON.

PLATES XX.—XXII.

The village of Thaon, in which is the fragment of a church delineated in the three *Plates XX.—XXII.*, is situated about ten miles north-east of Caen. As a specimen of genuine Norman architecture, this building

[1] *Architectural Antiquities of Normandy,* vol. ii. p. 60.

cannot fail to engage the attention of the antiquary. It consists of a nave and choir, divided by a central tower which rises through the roof of the church, with two stories, the lower one partially concealed by the nave and choir roofs. From the engraved plans, elevations, sections, and details, the reader will be able to understand the whole characteristic features of this building. It will be seen that the walls, to the west of the tower between columns, are additions to the original design, as it may be inferred that the arches on each side were formerly open to aisles. Mr. Cotman intimates that there was only a south aisle; but the accompanying plan shows that there are columns and arches on both sides. Externally these arches are plain, and without any ornaments or mouldings;[1] while internally they are adorned with three rows of zigzag, or chevron (see *Plate XXI*. No. 3.) In the interior the clerestory window is bounded by a string-moulding, which forms a hood to the arch, and extends round the whole church. The exterior of the western and eastern ends are shown at Nos. 1 and 2 on the same Plates, as well as the section of the walls and some of the details, more at large. The flat buttresses, arcades without columns, the small windows, also without columns or ornamental dressings—are all evidences of a simple and systematic style of architecture; and the experienced antiquary will not fail to perceive an analogy between the east end and the chancel of Barfreston Church, in Kent.[2] In both these edifices early pointed or lancet windows are introduced. There will also be found a coincidence in the nave of this church and that of St. Peter's at Northampton; particularly in the range of arcades and small windows to the clerestory, as well as in the block cornice, or corbel-table. These two English churches were raised, we have every reason to believe, soon after the Norman colonization of Britain. In *Plate XXII.*, the design, construction, and architectural character of the tower are clearly elucidated. The con-

[1] "On the corbels are not only represented grotesque heads, but some of the simplest heraldic charges—as the chief, chief indented, pale, bend, bendlets, undy, fess, saltier, crosses of various kinds, chevron, &c. Such ordinaries occasionally occur in similar situations on other Norman religious edifices, but only on the most ancient."—*Architectural Antiquities of Normandy*, vol. ii. p. 16.

[2] See *Architectural Antiquities of Great Britain*, for engravings and accounts of this building and of that at Northampton.

struction of its roof or pyramid will not escape the notice of the English antiquary, who will also examine the projecting heads at the angles of the roof, called crockets in Mr. Cotman's work.

CHURCH OF ST. LOUP, NEAR BAYEUX.

PLATE XXIII.

[This church belongs in its origin (according to De Caumont) to the Norman style of the twelfth century. The nave measures 69 feet long by 17 feet 9 inches wide. On the south wall are traces of two Norman arches with their voussoirs decorated with zigzags, which indicate (as well as the toothing left in the west façade wall) the former existence of a south aisle. It is not certain, however, whether this was ever built, though in a small chapel to the west of the tower is a piscina of sufficiently early date to warrant the supposition that the south wall of this chapel was the original aisle-wall. Externally also the masonry of the chapel bonds in with the Norman work of the tower. The archway opening to this chapel from the nave is fifteenth century, and has probably taken the place of a third Norman aisle arch. The choir, rebuilt in the thirteenth century, is 45 feet long by 20 feet wide, and at the west end of it are remains on either side of two transition doorways. The elegant tower, illustrated in *Plate XXIII.*, shows us an interesting and well-preserved specimen of Norman work, though various changes have considerably modified the primitive condition of the church to which it is attached. The tower is composed of three stories surmounted by a spire, whose stones are carved in imitation of shingles. On the west side is a doorway (fig. 3, *Plate XXIII.*) decorated with zigzags, and a bas-relief in the tympanum representing, according to the legend, the patron saint (St. Loup) subduing the dragon which devastated the country. This tower is placed at the south-east end of the nave, and on the opposite side of the latter is a fifteenth century chapel, 21 feet square.]

CATHEDRAL OF BAYEUX.

PLATES XXIV.—XXXIV.

Among the architectural antiquities of the famous city of Bayeux,[1] its cathedral is not only a prominent but a most important object. Occupying a sacred spot, which appears to have been dedicated to Christianity as early as the third century, it exhibits various styles and peculiarities of Norman and pointed architecture. [The history of the cathedral is as follows:—After the destruction of the building erected by Rollo, Bishop Hugues in the commencement of the eleventh century began a new church, dying, however, before it was completed. Odo, who succeeded him in 1050, continued the work, making considerable augmentations, and it was finished and dedicated in 1077, King William I. of England and his queen being present.] At the time of its dedication Odo enriched the church with various gifts, one of which was of peculiar value and splendour. This was a sort of chandelier, in the shape of a crown, composed of wood and copper, and covered with silver plates. It measured 16 feet in height by 38 feet in diameter;—was diversified with ornaments in the shape of crowns or towers, and was intended to hold "an immense number of tapers," or candles, which were lighted on high festivals. It was suspended from the roof in the nave, opposite the great crucifix, and is said to have continued there till 1562, when the Huguenots committed havoc in the church. If, however, the building was destroyed in the time of Henry I., it is not likely that this sumptuous ornament was saved. [In 1106 the cathedral was burned by the soldiers of Henry I. of England. On the termination of the war in 1107, it was restored by Henry, and remained in this state until 1159,

[1] The history of this city is intimately connected with that of England. It was here that Duke William, on being nominated by Edward the Confessor his successor to the English crown, caused Harold to attend and do him homage in the name of the nation. Here, also, Henry I. was detained prisoner by his eldest brother; in revenge for which, on coming to the throne, he laid siege to the city and burned it. (See *Archeologia*, vol. xvii. p. 911.) Again, Edward III. attacked and nearly destroyed Bayeux in 1356. Henry VI. brought from this city a large collection of Norman charters, which are now preserved in the Tower of London. The *Bayeux Tapestry* is a relic of great importance as an historical document.

when it was again burnt. To these two constructions of Odo and Henry I. may be attributed all that is Norman in the cathedral, viz. the nave arcades, the towers of the west front up to the base of the spires, and the lower portion of the central tower. (It is possible that the crypt, with its Roman groined vault and classic capitals, belong to the early construction of Bishop Hugues. The capitals certainly resemble more their classic prototypes than those of the crypt of the Abbaye aux Dames, which date from 1064).[1] The level of the pavement of the ancient church was about 4 feet below the present one, the choir being raised 3 feet above the nave. After the fire of 1159, Philippe de Harcourt, Bishop of Bayeux (1142–1164), strenuously set to work on the reconstruction of the present cathedral; and his successor, Henry of Salisbury (1165–1205), continued the works, which were terminated by Robert des Ablèges (1205–1231).

Between 1161 and 1231 were built the upper part of the nave with the side aisles (excepting the side chapels), the whole of the choir with its radiating chapels (including the lady chapel), and the sacristy of two stories. To the same period belongs also the masonry, which enveloped the nave-piers as well as the delicate capitals surmounting them, and the Norman sculptured arches. In fact, the surface decoration on the stone of the tympana and archivolts differs essentially from the older work. The stones have not been touched since they were first laid, but the parts added have been made to agree, and now present similarity of workmanship with that of the side aisles in the Gothic style. The mouldings of the circular-headed arches are the same as those of the pointed arches which cover the side aisles of the nave. The sculpture of the capitals also shows remarkable coincidences in the form, finish, and execution of its work with that of the rest of the construction.

The chapter-house, some of the chapels to the south of the nave, and perhaps also the north transept, are the work of the end of the thirteenth century. At the same time the north tower of the west front was strengthened by additions and restorations in the pointed style, in order to render it capable of carrying the spire with which it was terminated.

[1] [See Plates III. IV. and XXXI.–XXXIV.]

These constructions mask the external Norman work up to one-third of its height.

In the fourteenth century the other chapels of the nave were erected, the south tower spire, the south transept, and the masonry enveloping the piers of the transept. This latter work was executed not only to modify the Norman parts of the church, whose simplicity clashed with the luxury of the later additions, but also to give to those piers that extra strength necessary to support the weight of a central tower more important than that which then existed. The ancient piers of Odo's church became, therefore, the newels of the new piers, and it seems, from excavations lately made, that the foundations of the parts added were laid on the débris filled up round the old piers, and without going down to the foundations of these latter on *terra firma*. At this period were rebuilt all the lower arcades near these central piers, excepting those on the side of the choir. The great Norman arcades also of the central tower, too low in comparison with the rest of the new work, were replaced by others of pointed form, cut out in the wall of the Norman tower, and with their springing 13 feet above that of the Norman arches.

Toward the end of the fourteenth century, the interior of the church was, generally, in the same condition as previous to the restoration in 1855; in succeeding ages slight modifications had been made, such as restorations caused by the discovery of the ancient crypt in 1512, and alterations in the windows of the nave-chapels. In the fifteenth century (1425-27) the central tower, for which the piers had been strengthened, was erected by Monsignor Hubert; and fifty years afterwards the beautiful octagonal lantern which now exists was erected by Louis de Harcourt, Bishop of Bayeux, at a cost of £4092, 12s. 6d. Louis de Harcourt seems to have had some fear for the stability of the edifice, from the fact of his taking care to state that he should not feel himself responsible if the tower fell down, in consequence of the additional weight piled upon it:—"Ne si (quod Deus avertat) ex hâc dicta superedificatione aliquid ruinæ in posterum contingeret sibi et suæ huic devotioni quoquomodo valeat imputari."

This octagonal lantern was crowned with a cupola of wood framing

CATHEDRAL OF BAYEUX. 59

and lead, which was destroyed by fire in 1676; and in 1714, a new cupola in stone, crowned by a small lantern with Roman Doric columns, was erected by the architect Moussard: excepting in detail, it accorded very fairly with the rest of the work.

These subsequent additions, however, very nearly led to the total ruin of the central tower. As far back as the fifteenth century, and prior to Louis de Harcourt's erection, great cracks had become visible in the four central and side piers, and in 1714, Moussard had deemed it expedient to modify his original design (his lantern was to have been 17 feet higher) in order not to increase them. Many attempts were made to persuade the existing government of France to undertake the restoration of the tower, but in vain, until by command of the Emperor Napoleon III., M. Flachat (from whose work we have abridged this description) was instructed to report upon the state of the cathedral. For a description of the restoration, which was commenced towards the close of 1855, we must refer the reader to his work[1] (published in conjunction with M. Dion), which contains the most complete account of the extraordinary means it was found requisite to adopt, in order to support the central tower (weighing upwards of 4000 tons) whilst the ruinous piers were being removed and rebuilt.

The works were completed in 1863, costing upwards of £15,000, which was defrayed chiefly by the emperor, out of his civil list. The only difference in the appearance of the work now completed lies in the cupola, which has been built in a style more in accordance with the tower beneath it; Moussard's cupola having been pulled down in 1855.]

Plate XXIV. is a valuable ground plan of the church, with its series of chapels, &c.; the dimensions of which in French feet are thus stated by Béziers:—Height of the central tower. 224 feet; of the two western ditto, 230 feet; length of the interior of the church, 296 feet; width of ditto, 76 feet; height of ditto, 76 feet; length of the nave, 140 feet; width of the nave, 38 feet; ditto of side aisles, 17 feet; ditto of chapels, 15 feet; length of the transepts, 113 feet; width of ditto, 33 feet; length of the

[1 Dion (A. de Laurent) and Flachat (E.), *Cathedral de Bayeux*, 1861, Paris, 4to.]

choir, 118 feet; width of ditto, 36 feet. Its measurements in English feet may be ascertained by the scale on the engraved plan.

The elevation of the west front (*Plate XXV, XXVI.*) shows an interesting portion of the edifice. The lower part of the front is occupied by a screen, divided into five compartments, with pointed arches. The several orders of the arches, and the inclosed tympana, are richly decorated with historical sculpture.

In the two exterior compartments the arches are unpierced, and are flanked by a profusion of clustered columns: over each of the four lateral arches are gables, crocketed, the tympana of which are pierced by a variety of quatrefoils, trefoils, and other ornaments, within circular mouldings. Above the central arch is a flat balustrade of quatrefoils, behind which rises a large pointed window, of very rich tracery. Over this window is a row of statues of saints, placed in niches, and arranged in pairs, with a highly-pointed gable above each pair. [The two flanking towers are bold and massive, the casing of the lower portion adding considerably to this effect; the circular windows or openings of the original towers are still visible here and there, and the upper story retains its Norman features, the three circular-headed windows which are of great beauty of proportion and detail.] The towers have fine corbel tables and are surmounted by spires of very ancient date, at the bases of which spring pinnacles of corresponding design.

The exterior of the nave presents a specimen of the ornamented pointed style, whilst the pointed architecture of the choir is elegant and simple. An elevation of the exterior of one of the compartments of the choir shown on *Plate XXXIII, XXXIV.*, will convey a clear idea of the execution of the whole design: but even in this part there is a want of uniformity; some of the windows are deeply imbedded in the walls, whilst others are nearly on a level with the surface. The southern portal is bold and appropriate, though not in the purest style. On each side of the doorway were originally three statues, whose tabernacles remain, though the saints have been unniched. Over the door is a bas-relief, containing numerous figures, disposed in three compartments, and representing some legendary tale or events, which it is not very easy to decipher.

The interior of the church consists of a nave, lateral aisles, and a transept, and a choir, with aisles and chapels. The six piers of the nave are massive, with clustered shafts. The arches above them are semi-circular, of four orders, the outer one enriched with the chevron moulding, diamonds, etc.; and examples occur of the square embattled, the lozenge, with acorns, the lotus, and leaves occupying the triangular interstices, and with other ornaments. On one of them is a curious border of heads with beards, and some with elongated and upright ears, and some with crowns. These and other specimens of the decorative mouldings are shown in Plate XXX. The wall above the arches is adorned with a species of tessellated work cut in the stone, of varied patterns, some interwoven, others reticulated: the lines indented in the stones, as well as the joints which form the patterns, are filled with a black cement, or mastic, so as to form a kind of *niello*. This may be seen in the Plate just referred to; where also the capitals of the pillars are shown to be an imitation of classic examples.

In the nave there is no triforium, but above the richly-decorated string-course or cornice of the lower story runs a light gallery, below the windows of the clerestory: the façade of this gallery consists of a range of trefoil-headed arches, with trefoils in the spandrils, and immediately below the corona, as well as under the cornice beneath, is a range of quatrefoils, as may be seen in *Plates XXVIII, XXIX.* and *XXX.* The windows of the clerestory are, in the opinion of Mr. Turner, the loftiest ever seen in a similar situation. The very tall arches that support the central tower are likewise pointed; as are those of the transept, the choir, the side-aisles, and the chapels. Of the choir, an elevation of the exterior and interior of one of the compartments may be seen in *Plate XXXIII, XXXIV.*, and a transverse section in *Plate XXXI, XXXII.* The capitals of the columns supporting the pointed arches bear some resemblance to those of the Norman pillars; and the spandrils are adorned with circular ornaments, having a resemblance to small rose-windows with their tracery. Some are merely in bas-relief; in others the central circles are deeply perforated, whilst the ribs are composed of delicate tracery. The triforium consists of a

Q

series of pointed arches, each inclosing a smaller pair under a larger one occupying the whole width of the lower arch: the clustered pillars have capitals, and the angles between the arches are occupied by trefoils, circles, and other delicate ornaments. The spandrils of the arches are relieved by circles with sculptured figures. Each of the three stories is separated from one another by a string-course of foliage, of very elegant design and execution. The stalls of the choir are beautifully executed in oak, and beneath them are misereres, variously carved. Upon the roof of the choir are still to be seen the portraits of the first twenty-one bishops of Bayeux, each with his name. The walls of the chapels of the choir were covered with large fresco paintings, now nearly obliterated. Indeed, the whole of the cathedral at one time displayed a profusion of works of art.

Beneath the choir is a subterraneous chapel, or crypt, dedicated to St. Manvieu, of a similar character to that of the Holy Trinity at Caen. The walls are covered with paintings, probably of the fifteenth century; but those upon the springing of the arches above the pillars appear to be considerably older. Over the only window that gives light to this crypt, is preserved an inscription to the memory of Bishop de Boissy.

The canons of this place once possessed the celebrated piece of needle-work, now known as the *Bayeux Tapestry*, but heretofore as the "Toile de St. Jean." Since the time it was unrolled and publicly exhibited[1] by Bonaparte, it has been kept at the hôtel of the prefecture. This interesting tapestry, the work of Queen Matilda, has been amply illustrated in the *Archæologia*, and *Vetusta Monumenta*, of the Society of Antiquaries. [A very careful and elaborate series of photographs, coloured after the original, has since been made; it was exhibited in the International Exhibition at South Kensington, and belongs to the department of Science and Art.]

[1] The Tapestry was publicly exhibited throughout the large provincial towns of France, in order to incite the people to war with England.]

CHURCH OF ST. PETER, CAEN.

PLATES XXXV. AND *XXXVI.*

St. Regnobert, who preached the gospel to the Saxons in the seventh century, is supposed to have been the original founder of a church on the site of the present one dedicated to St. Peter.[1] The present edifice is the work of various ages. The choir and a part of the nave were erected very late in the thirteenth century; and the remainder of the nave and the bell-tower were built in 1308. Mr. Turner says, that "the tower and spire were built in the year 1308, under the direction of Nicolle *l'Anglois*, a burgher of Caen, and treasurer of the church." Ducarel asserts, from the name, that he was a native of England. The portal under the tower, which is of the date of 1384,[2] was restored and ornamented with statues in 1608; and it has undergone some alterations in modern times, not at all to the improvement of the original work. Here were to be seen many bas-reliefs, representing memorable events in the history of St. Peter, which, says De la Rue, were defaced by the Vandals of 1793.[3]

The north aisle of the nave was erected in 1410, and the south aisle some years afterwards. The apse of the choir, and the vaulted roof of the choir and of its aisles, were executed by Hector Sohier, architect of Caen, in 1521.[4]

The elevation, section, and plans of the tower and spire, *Plate XXXV, XXXVI.*, will furnish every information as to the design, style, and architectural features of this portion of the building. The doorway is finished by a lofty gable of the altitude of half of the second story, and is pierced by three windows, and has two niches, under an arch moulding. Over it, and in the tympanum of the gable, is another niche, of plain workmanship. The remainder of the second story is relieved by a series of blank arcades with gable ends, their tympanums

---

[1] De la Rue, *Essais*, &c., tome i. p. 95.
[2] In a record of the year 1384, the great entrance is called the "*Portail Neuf.*" Ib. p. 96.
[3] Ut supra.
[4] Huet, *Orig. de Caen*, p. 193.

being occupied by trefoils. A string-course of quatrefoil in panel divides it from the next story, which consists of lancet-arches, some glazed and others blank, of very elaborate workmanship. This is crowned by an open parapet of quatrefoil, which is adorned at each angle and in the centre with pinnacles, having niches for statues, &c. The spire, which is very lofty, is pierced by trefoils, quatrefoils, and other similar openings, distributed in alternate compartments, the intermediate spaces being occupied by broad bands of several rows of the dog-tooth ornament. On this tower and spire Mr. Turner remarks (vol. ii. p. 178):—"The elevation is hardly inferior to that of the spire of Salisbury Cathedral.[1] Elegance, lightness, and symmetry are the general characters of the whole, though the spire has peculiar characters of its own."

A wooden door from this church is shown in *Plate LXIX*. No. 2. It is very plain, and divided horizontally into two compartments, distributed into panels with trefoil-headed arches, within ogee arches crocketed. Those of the upper compartment are gabled; and the whole of the panels are separated by plain buttresses, terminated by pinnacles.

DUCAL PALACE, CAEN.

PLATE XXXVII.

[This building, better known under the name of the "Salle des Gardes," is attached to the Ecole Normale, Caen, and is at present used as a gymnasium. It dates from the early part of the fourteenth century,

[1] This opinion may be adduced as one of the instances of the erroneous inferences we are liable to in judging of the relative heights of objects, without taking pains to form something like a scale. By the figured measures on the engraving it will be seen that the whole altitude of the tower and spire of St. Peter's is only 242 English feet, whereas that of Salisbury is 404 feet from the floor. Of the comparative beauty in proportions of the two towers and spires, I must differ in opinion from my esteemed friend; he giving the preference to St. Peter's, I to that of Salisbury. In the former the spire is too large and heavy. It should be remarked, that the tower of St. Peter's is seen to rise immediately from the ground—whereas that of Salisbury is only seen above the roof of the church. [Salisbury tower (upper portion only), and spire were erected in 1331.—*Rickman*.]

and formed part of the ancient "Abbaye aux Hommes." The ground floor is vaulted, the vault being carried by two rows of columns: this portion is now divided up by a series of walls. The upper part, used as the gymnasium, is a magnificent hall 104 ft. long by 31 ft. wide, and 26 ft. 6 in. up to the tie-beams of the roof. The floor was at one time decorated with glazed tiles, many of which are still preserved in the Antiquaries' Museum and the Town Library. This hall is now ceiled at the level of the tie-beams, the space in the roof being used as a granary. Traces of painted decoration of the fourteenth century are still visible in the roof. Small staircases at the four angles of the building formerly led to the roof for repairs or in case of fire, and a fine staircase to the north-east of the building is supposed by M. Bouet to have led to the main floor of the hall. A restoration of this staircase (exterior perspective only) is given in the *Institute Transactions*, illustrating Mr. Parker's paper, read Jan. 26, 1863, and the same woodcut is also to be found in M. Bouet's work on the abbey.[1] M. Bouet remarks[2] that he has restored the roofs of the four turrets in stone, as in Pugin's plate, but that he believes they were originally in wood; at all events they were destroyed in 1684.]

CHURCH OF ST. OUEN, ROUEN.

PLATES XXXVIII.—XLIII.

Among the numerous specimens of splendid ecclesiastical architecture in Normandy and other parts of France, the Church of St. Ouen ranks pre-eminent. From its richness of decoration, its exuberance of fancy, and its elaborate execution, it cannot fail to attract the attention and admiration of all travellers, and must prove peculiarly interesting to the architectural antiquary. Although the accompanying Plates (*XXXVIII.—XLIII.*) do not constitute a complete illustration of the church, they will serve to show its prevailing features, and furnish the

[[1] *Analyse architecturale de l'Abbaye de Saint Etienne de Caen*, p. 98.   [2] P. 99.]

artist with materials for practical purposes or historical inference. The foundation of the present building was laid in 1318 by the Abbot Jean Roussel, better known by the name of *Marc d'argent*, by whom it was advanced as far as the transept; the remainder was the work of subsequent periods, and the building was continued to the beginning of the sixteenth century;—it is not even now completed. [According to Mr. Fergusson (*Hist. Arch.*) the work of building "was carried on uninterruptedly for twenty-one years by Marc d'argent. At his death the choir and transepts were completed, or very nearly so. The English wars interrupted at this time the progress of this, as of many other buildings; and the works of the nave were not seemingly resumed till about 1490, and twenty-five years later the beautiful west front was commenced." Mr. Fergusson goes on to say, "Except that of Limoges, the choir is almost the most perfect building of its age; and being contemporary with the choir at Cologne (1276–1321), affords a means of comparison between the two styles of Germany and France at that age, and entirely to the advantage of the French example, which, though very much smaller, avoids all the more glaring faults of the other.

Nothing indeed can exceed the beauty of proportion of this most elegant church; and except that it wants the depth and earnestness of the earlier examples, it may be considered as the most beautiful thing of its kind in Europe. The proportion too of the nave, transepts, and choir to one another is remarkably happy, and a most striking contrast to the very imperfect proportions of Cologne. Its three towers, also, would have formed a perfect group as originally designed; but the central one was not completed till so late that its details have lost the aspiring character of the building on which it stands, and the western spires, as rebuilt within the last ten years, are incongruous and inappropriate; whereas had the original design been carried out according to the drawings which still exist,[1] it would have been one of the most beautiful façades known anywhere. The diagonal position of the towers

[1 The west front was terminated (1846–52) by the addition of two flanking steeples, surmounting three deep-set portals, but effecting a change from the original design, which is preserved in the Town Library.—(*Murray*).]

met most happily the difficulty of giving breadth to the façade, without placing them beyond the line of the aisles, as is done in the cathedral of Rouen, and at the same time gave a variety to the perspective which must have had the most pleasing effect. Had the idea occurred earlier, few western towers would have been placed otherwise; but the invention came too late, and in modern times the very traces of the arrangement have been obliterated."]

The *ground plan* (*Plate XXXVIII.*) gives an idea of the extent and dimensions of the church;[1] and the view of the nave, looking east (*Plate XXXIX.*) shows the impressive perspective of the interior. The arches of the interior are of great height and fine proportions, and its entire aspect is excessively light and lofty; the mouldings of the arches are shallow, and the building seems all window. The lightness of effect is considerably aided by the clerestory gallery opening to the glazed tracery of the windows, behind, the mullions of the one corresponding with those of the other. To each of the clustered columns of the nave are attached two tabernacles, consisting of canopies and pedestals, for the reception of statues of saints. These are shown in the interior view, and also in the elevation and section of one of the compartments of the nave. *Plate XL.* The pillars of the choir do not appear to have been similarly ornamented; but upon one of them, serving as a corbel to a truncated column, is a head of our Saviour, and on the opposite pillar, another of the Virgin; the former exhibiting a remarkably fine antique character.

The capitals of the pillars in the choir were formerly gilt, and the spandrils of the arches painted with angels—now nearly effaced. Round the choir, as shown in the plan, is a series of chapels, or oratories, the walls of which have been covered with fresco paintings of figures and foliage. In the chapel of St. Agnes is an inscribed stone commemorating the melancholy death of Alexander Berneval, the master mason of the building, who, it is traditionally said, murdered his apprentice from jealousy, he having executed the very splendid *circular window* in the

[1] The following are the dimensions of the interior in French feet, as given in Mr. Turner's Tour:— Length of the church, 416 ft.; ditto, nave, 231 ft.; ditto, choir, 108 ft.; ditto, lady chapel, 66 ft.; ditto, transept, 130 ft.; width of ditto, 34 ft.; ditto, nave without the aisles, 34 ft.; ditto, including aisles, 78 ft.; height of roof, 100 ft.; ditto, of tower, 240 ft.

northern transept, which is generally allowed to be superior to that on the southern side, which was the workmanship of the envious master. This window exhibits in its tracery the produced pentagon, or combination of triangles, called the pentalpha. These large circular windows, sometimes known by the name of rose or marigold windows, are beautiful characteristic features of French ecclesiastical architecture. In this church, besides those in the transepts, there is a very fine specimen in the great west window, which is fully delineated in *Plates XLII. XLIII.*

The flying-buttresses end in richly crocketed pinnacles, supported by shafts of unusual height; one of them is shown in *Plate XL.* with the section of a compartment of the nave. The triple tiers of windows seem to have occupied nearly all the wall work of the building. Balustrades of various quatrefoils run round the aisles and body. The centre tower, which is wholly composed of open arches and tracery, terminates, like the south tower of Rouen Cathedral, with an octangular crown of fleurs-de-lis. The elegance of the south porch and transept is unrivalled. This portion of the church was always finished with care: it was the scene of many religious ceremonies, particularly of espousals. The bold and lofty entrance of this porch is surrounded within by pendent trefoil arches, springing from carved bosses, and forming an open festoon of tracery. The vaulting within is ribbed, and ornamented with richly carved pendants, and the portal, which it shades, is covered with a profusion of sculpture: the death, entombment, and apotheosis of the Virgin, form the principal groups. Mr. Turner considers them, both in design and execution, far superior to any specimens of the corresponding era in England. On the same side of the church is an interesting *doorway*, a representation of which is given in *Plate XLI.* It exhibits an arch of late flamboyant form, richly crocketed, and terminating in a finial of very beautiful design, and a pointed arch similarly ornamented with crockets, and the mouldings decorated by a continued range of vine leaves, which descends some way down the jambs.

Several specimens of painted glass from this church are engraved (*Plates LXXVII. LXXVIII.*), to show the design. It is a singular but a happy circumstance, that the church preserves the whole of its original glazing. Each intermullion contains one whole-length figure, represented upon a diapered ground, good in design, though the artist seems to have avoided the employment of brilliant hues. The sober light harmonizes with the gray, unsullied stone work, and gives a most pleasing unity of tint to the receding arches.

CHURCH OF ST. VINCENT, ROUEN.

PLATES XLIV. XLV.

[The most remarkable part of this church is the western porch, of which we give illustrations in *Plates XLIV.* and *XLV.* The centre and side archways, which are unusually lofty in proportion to their width, have a few simple mouldings, with foliage and a crocketed ogee label. The intrados of the arch is richly decorated with trefoiled cusps, which extend some 5 feet below the springing. This archway is flanked by buttresses richly adorned with niches, and canopies surmounted by elaborate crocketed pinnacles. The plan of the porch is very curious, reminding us somewhat of that at Ratisbon Cathedral, except that here there are three archways instead of two only, as in the latter example. The two side archways are placed at an obtuse angle with the central one, so as to form, as it were, a more easy access to those who approached it from the north or south: the porch of St. Maclou has a somewhat similar arrangement. The outer order of the doorway to the church is decorated with a series of seated statues with canopies over them, and the tympanum is filled with a bas-relief, somewhat mutilated, and apparently representing the last judgment. Much of the rest of the church is posterior to the sixteenth century. The east end is now undergoing restoration; a new chapel and a "sacristie" being added. The church contains much fine glass.]

NUNNERY OF ST. CLAIR, ROUEN.

PLATE XLVI.

[This convent was founded in 1481 by Jean d'Estonville, and dedicated to the Holy Virgin and St. John Baptist. Its architecture, with the exception of the entrance doorway (an illustration of which we give in *Plate XLVI.*), is not of any great note; the form of arch, however, is interesting from the contrast it presents to our four-centred arch of English work of the same period, or a little later; the crown of the arch, it will be observed, is segmental and struck from one centre instead of two as in England; a four-centred arch is very rare in France, and in fact it frequently happens, when a relieving arch is formed over the doorway, as in this instance, that the crown of the lower arch is horizontal, with voussoirs radiating to a centre; the extreme ends on either side being semicircular. The tomb of the founder, who died in 1484, lies in the centre of the church.]

FOUNTAIN DE LA CROSSE, ROUEN.

PLATE XLVII.

This fountain, so called from its proximity to a house where formerly hung as a sign the crosier belonging to the monks of Notre Dame de l'Ile Dieu, is situated in the Rue de l'Hôpital.[1] It is an interesting specimen of the architecture of the fifteenth century. Its general design may be understood by referring to *Plate XLVII.*, which shows a plan, an elevation, and details. The fountain projects from a wall like a bow-window, and its sides are richly decorated with niches surmounted by rich canopies of fanciful tracery. The fountain has a concave pyramidal

[1] Rouen is noted for the number of its fountains, there being not less than thirty for the use of the public, supplied with water from five different springs, and conveyed into the city by canals.

cover in stone, which in Millin's time was surmounted by a royal crown. [The fountain has been restored, or rather rebuilt, within the last ten years.]

FOUNTAIN DE LA CROIX DE PIERRE, ROUEN.

PLATE XLVIII.

This fountain stands at the junction of three streets, in the Carrefour St. Vivienne, which, previous to the reign of St. Louis, were without the walls of the city. [It was erected in the year 1500, under the auspices of the Cardinal d'Amboise, whose tomb lies in the cathedral, and has some resemblance to the crosses erected to the memory of Queen Eleanor, in England.] As shown in the plans and elevation, *Plate XLVIII.*, it consists of three stories, of varied design, raised on a plain basement. In the first and second stories are canopied niches, with pedestals, &c. [This fountain is being rebuilt on the original model: the old one being too much dilapidated to allow of any partial restoration.]

THE PALAIS DE JUSTICE, ROUEN.

PLATES XLIX.—LIV.

In this interesting edifice the three estates composing the Duchy of Normandy—viz. the deputies of the church, the nobility, and the good towns—formerly held their meetings. Here, also, the Court of Exchequer had its sittings. Where the states once deliberated, the electors of the department now assemble, for the purpose of naming the deputies who represent them in the great council of the nation. The palace, in its present state, is composed of three distinct buildings, erected at different times, and forming collectively three sides of a parallelogram, whose fourth side is merely an embattled wall, with an elaborate gateway. One of these buildings, named the *Salle des Procureurs*, was erected in 1497, six years anterior to that more properly called the *Palais de Justice*, but was subsequently annexed to the palace. The exterior of the *Salle des Procureurs*,[1] the south elevation of which, with a ground plan and section, are shown on *Plate XLIX*., is comparatively simple: the most highly decorated part of it is the gable, which is flanked by two octangular turrets, shown in the same Plate. The roof is of a very high pitch, in which are dormer windows, of rich execution. Between the square windows, in the body of the hall, are buttresses with tracery.

The interior is a fine large hall, with a wooden roof boarded under the braces. It is 150 feet long and 50 feet wide, and now serves the same purpose as our Westminster Hall, viz. a *salle des pas-perdus:* beneath the hall is a prison.

The southern building, erected exclusively for the sittings of the Exchequer, is very sumptuous in its decorations, both without and within. Here the windows in the body of the building have flattened elliptical heads; and are divided by a mullion and a transom. The mouldings are highly wrought and enriched with foliage, and are nearly counterparts of those in the château at Fontaine le Henri. The dormer windows, vieing with those in the Place de la Pucelle, are of a different design, and form the most characteristic feature of the front: they are pointed, and enriched with mullions and tracery, and are placed within triple canopies of nearly the same form, flanked by square pillars, terminating in tall crocketed pinnacles; some of them are fronted with open arches, crowned with statues. A most superb specimen may be seen on reference to the engraved Plate of the elevation, section, and plan of the south front, *Plate XLIX.*, and the other print, *Plate LI.*, which must be valuable to the architect. A polygonal bay-window, of highly enriched workmanship, projects into the court, and varies the elevation. Much of the interest of the Palais de Justice has been destroyed by its not having been allowed to continue in its original state; for one half of it has been degraded by

[1 Built originally as an exchange for native and foreign merchants.]

alterations, or stripped of its ornaments. The room in which the parliament formerly met, and which is now employed for the trial of criminal causes, still remains comparatively uninjured.[1] Its ceiling of oak, nearly as black as ebony, divided into numerous compartments, and covered with a profusion of carving and gilt ornaments, affords a gorgeous example of the taste of the times when constructed. The open-work bosses of this ceiling are gone, as are the doors enriched with sculpture, and the ancient chimney-piece, and the escutcheons charged with sacred devices, and the great painting by which, before the Revolution, witnesses were made to swear. Around the apartment are several sentences, in letters of gold, reminding judges, jurors, witnesses, and suitors, of their duties. [The ancient wainscotting round the room, painted over with arabesques and old mottoes, has since been taken down or effaced by whitewash.] The room itself is said to be the most beautiful in France for its proportions and quantity of light. [A new wing in the style of the rest of the building has been erected opposite to the *Salle des Procureurs*, thus completing three sides of the great court, the fourth side being inclosed by railings.]

HÔTEL DE BOURGTHEROULDE, ROUEN.

PLATES LV. LVI.

In the *Place de la Pucelle d'Orleans* is a large house of stone, &c., partly of the same era as the Palais de Justice, but richer in its sculptures. It is the only house of the kind remaining at Rouen, and may be regarded as the most curious specimen of domestic architecture in Normandy. This hôtel was erected in 1506 by Guillaume de Roux, the twelfth of that name, Lord of Bourgtheroulde, and finished in 1537 by his son the Abbé d'Aumale, whose arms are emblazoned in various parts of the edifice. The entire front is divided into compartments by slender

[1] Since this was written the whole ceiling has been restored by M. Viollet le Duc.]

buttresses or pilasters. The intervening spaces are filled with bas-reliefs, evidently executed by different masters; and there is not a single square foot of this extraordinary building which has not been ornamented.

The principal façade of the court, represented in *Plate LV.*, is also decorated with bas-reliefs, very rich in their composition and execution, which extend under all the windows of the first story, and also below those of the upper tier. A banquet beneath a window in the first floor is in a good *cinque-cento* style. Others represent the labours of the field and the vineyard, fishing, &c.; all are rich and fanciful in costume. The salamander, the emblem of Francis I., appears several times very conspicuously amongst the ornaments. Many of the bas-reliefs are engraved and minutely described by E. H. Langlois in his *Description Historique des Maisons de Rouen*. On the north side, and joining the octagonal tower, extends a spacious gallery, the architecture of which is rather in Holbein's manner. Foliaged and swelling pilasters, like antique candelabra, decorate the jambs of the windows. Beneath is the well-known series of bas-reliefs, executed on marble tablets, representing the interview between Francis I. of France and Henry VIII. of England, in the Champ du Drap d'Or, between Guisnes and Ardres; the heads of these kings are placed within two niches on each side of the gateway entering the court. They were first discovered by the venerable Father Montfaucon, who had them engraved for his *Monumens de la Monarchie Française*. These sculptures are much mutilated, and so obscured by smoke and dirt, that the details cannot be easily understood. The corresponding tablets, above the windows, are even in a worse condition, and appear to have been almost unintelligible in the time of Montfaucon, who conjectured that they were allegorical, and intended to represent the triumph of religion. Each tablet contains a triumphal car, drawn by different animals, and crowded with mythological figures and attributes. The finial of one of the tower roofs is composed of a group of leaden thistles, which has proved a puzzle to antiquaries. (See *Plate LV.* B.)

[Very little now (1874) remains of the external elevation, a small drawing of which is given in *Plate LVI.*; the corner turret fell down some twenty years ago, and about that time the entrance doorway was refaced with stone, with the intention of copying the ancient flamboyant ornamental details; this, however, has not yet been done, so that the stone is left in block. The rest of the building is in very fair condition.]

THE ABBEY ST. AMAND, ROUEN.

PLATES LVII. LVIII.

Whatever may have been the character and beauty of this building originally, very little now remains, and that is of comparatively modern date. [The earliest monastery was a dependency of St. Ouen; and was several times devastated. It was founded in 1030, destroyed by fire in 1126 and in 1562, and ceased to exist as a monastic establishment in 1569.] The illustrations in *Plates LVII.* and *LVIII.* represent the style of decoration prevailing in the house which belonged to the abbess, and which is in a great degree in ruins. What remains, however, is very curious; and is perhaps the oldest specimen of domestic architecture in Rouen. It is partly of wood, the front carved with arches and other sculpture in bas-relief, and partly of stone. The building surrounds a courtyard, at one angle of which is a polygonal turret, with the arms of the abbess, Marie d'Annebaut, who governed here in 1532. The northern side of the court was built at the end of the fifteenth century, under the abbacy of Thomasse Daniel. The façade, except the ground floor, is entirely of timber, richly adorned with panels, tracery, &c., and with windows of painted glass. On the first story is a room having two chimneys, with a ceiling of timber, divided into squares and painted scroll-work. The whole of this apartment is decorated with carvings, executed with the greatest delicacy. The mantle-piece of one of the fireplaces is imitative of a hurdle, and has the arms of the Daniels, much mutilated. The whole is crowned by a frieze of arabesques, in the midst of which are the arms of Guillemette d'Assy, who was abbess in

1518. The mantle-piece, also similarly charged, has columns decorated with capitals, singularly composed of heads of cherubim. The gateway to this ancient abbey, which was founded in 1030, was in the Rue St. Amand, near the parish church, and opposite the Rue de la Chaîne. It is of the time of Louis XIV., was built in the ancient walls of the convent, and is now in the same state as it was in 1792. [The abbey is now occupied by the Hotel St. Amand, Rue Imperiale, No. 35. Mr. W. Burges, in his folio of architectural drawings, gives a Plate representing the wainscotting which lined one of the rooms in this abbey, and makes the following remarks: "Until late years the buildings of the Abbey of St. Amand presented three objects of interest to the student. The first was a wooden house, the timbers of which were carved into buttresses, pinnacles, and mouldings, and carved tracery panels were employed for the filling in" (illustrated in *Plate LVII.*). "This building, I believe, still exists.[1] The second object was a beautiful tourelle of the very best time of the Renaissance.... The third thing was a room entirely lined with wainscotting.... On the chimney occurred the arms of Guillemette d'Assy, 1518; but on the painting are those of the house of Souvré, of which there were no less than three abbesses, a long time after Guillemette d'Assy. For this reason, E. H. Langlois (*Maisons de Rouen*) thinks that the painting must be far later than the wainscotting; but after all, these arms might merely indicate a renewal of the colours on the rails and stiles, as these latter were found eventually to have been several times repainted. In 1853, almost immediately after my visit, the place was destroyed, to make room for a new wide street. The wooden house still remains, but the tourelle and panelling were bought by a speculating builder, who has put them up in a modern suburban villa, where they were to be seen a few years ago, restored and spoiled."]

[1] The piercing of the Rue Imperiale (now Rue de la République), and the rebuilding of the houses on a larger scale in consequence, has almost destroyed the whole of this very fine timber façade.]

THE CATHEDRAL OF NOTRE DAME, ROUEN.

PLATES LIX.–LXII.

The date of the foundation is uncertain, but an edifice was built on this site in 1063, when Duke William attended at the dedication. [M. Viollet le Duc says (*Dict. Raisonné*, vol. ii. p. 361), "The Cathedral of Rouen, already in the twelfth century occupied all the ground it now covers. Rebuilt for the third time during the eleventh century, it was again reconstructed during the second half of the twelfth century in the transition style. Of these constructions there remains only the tower called St. Romain, on the north side of the western porch, the two apsidal chapels, those of the transepts, and the two doorways of the façade, opening into the nave aisles; these last portions would seem to belong to the end of the twelfth century. When Richard Cœur de Lion died, therefore, in 1199, the cathedral occupied the whole of the present site. Shortly after the seizure of Normandy by Philip Augustus in 1204, and its union to the crown of France, great works were undertaken; the nave, transepts and choir were rebuilt after a fire which probably damaged considerably the twelfth-century church. Towards the end of the thirteenth century chapels were built between the buttresses of the nave aisles. In 1302 was commenced the reconstruction of the Lady Chapel on a larger scale than the twelfth-century chapel previously existing; and about this period the two gables of the north and south transepts (portail de la Calende et portail des Libraires) were reconstructed. These works of the beginning of the fourteenth century surpass both in richness of design and beauty of execution all we know of the same kind and belonging to this period. In 1430 the windows of the choir were enlarged to obtain more light, and the windows of the nave, a considerable portion of the exterior cornices, &c., and the interior galleries were also modified during the fifteenth century. In 1485 was commenced the construction of the tower known as the *tour de Beurre*, and in 1509 the Cardinal Georges d'Amboise commenced the reconstruction of the western façade, which has never been completed. In the thirteenth century, on the pillars of the intersection of nave and transept, there existed already a lofty square tower, of which two stories still remain. These were injured by the wind in 1353, repaired afterward, and burned in 1514. They were a second time restored, and surmounted with an immense flêche or spire of wood, covered with lead, which was completed in 1544. This spire was destroyed by lightning in 1821;" and we regret to say replaced by one of the most hideous features ever conceived—a cast-iron spire, inclined out of the perpendicular, and still wanting some 20 feet more in height and a finial to complete it.] In 1538 Cardinal Georges d'Amboise, the great benefactor, restored the roof of the choir, which had been injured in 1514 by the destruction of the spire.]

On the northern side of the cathedral is the *cloister-court*, only a few arches of which now remain. This appears on the eastern side to have consisted of a double aisle or ambulatory. In *Plate LXVI.* is engraved one of the doorways on the north side of this cloister, and it will be found to be an interesting specimen. From a series of small clustered columns rises a pointed arch, richly ornamented, and decorated with crockets. The doors are square-headed, and divided by a pier or cluster-column (*trumeau*), and the upper part of the arch is filled up and relieved by trefoils and a quatrefoil, in which, from a sculptured bracket, rises a headless saint, holding a book. There is another saint on the apex of the arch, and two female figures are placed, one on each side, at the springing of the arch. The northern transept is approached through a gloomy court, once occupied by the shops of the transcribers and calligraphists, the *Libraires* of ancient times, and from them it has derived its name. The *Cour des Libraires* is entered beneath a gateway of beautiful and singular architecture, composed of two lofty pointed arches, of equal height, crowned by a row of smaller arcades; and is flanked by buttresses decorated with niches, with canopies and pediments, and other buttresses terminating in finials. One of the gateways is engraved in *Plate LXII.*, where are also some sections, plans, and mouldings, in detail; and in Plate *LXVIII.* a representation is given of one half of the wooden door, which is most highly adorned with panelling and tracery. The staircase in the north transept and adjoining the doorway is peculiarly delicate and beautiful (see *Plates LIX.* and *LX.*) Its date being well ascertained, we may note it as an architectural standard. It was erected by the Archbishop Cardinal d'Etouteville, about 1460, forty years subsequently to the building of the room above.

CHURCH OF ST. MICHAEL DE VAUCELLES, CAEN.

PLATE LXIII.

Vaucelles is at this time the largest of the five parishes composing the faubourgs of Caen, from which town it is separated by the canal of the Orne. Of the precise date of the church, which is situated on an eminence, forming a picturesque object in a distant view, we have no accurate information: it exhibits specimens of many of the styles of architecture which prevailed between the tenth and sixteenth centuries. The ancient tower, and the piers supporting it, belong to an ancient church of the eleventh or twelfth century. The tower is square and massy, and surmounted by a pyramidal stone roof or stunted spire. The basement story is plain, and only pierced by one single window of very small dimensions. A second story extends from the cornice of the body of the church to the pitch of the roof, and is decorated by small semicircular arches, without either mouldings or imposts. Each face of the upper story is occupied by a series of three long and narrow Norman arches, supported by columns having bases and capitals, as are those of the small round turret at the angle of the tower. It is probable that a part of the nave is of the same age as this tower, for some of the arches appear originally to have been of the semicircular form.[1] [The choir and chapels belong, according to De Caumont, to the fifteenth century, the nave and side aisles to the sixteenth, and the subsequent additions to the nave, the west façade, and a second tower, date from 1780.]

[1] A beautiful etching of this tower appears in Cotman's *Architectural Antiquities of Normandy.*

The north porch,[1] with the chapel attached to it, is an interesting and singular specimen of the decorative style of the latter part of the fourteenth century. *Plate LXIII.* represents an elevation of the front and flank, with measurements and some details. It is entered through a pointed arch elaborately decorated and having its inner archivolt fringed with pendant trefoils, a series of which adorn the two copings of the gable; the exterior corbel of the archivolt is crocketed, and finishes in a pinnacle, which serves for the base of a statue placed in the tympanum of the gable, which is filled in with flowing tracery. The pointed arch is flanked by graduated buttresses, cut into panels, decorated with tabernacle work, and surmounted by pinnacles, which in the Plate are restorations. The vaulting is ribbed; and the entrances into the church are by two flat elliptical arches under crocketed ogee canopies, between which is a piece of sculpture standing on a bold pedestal. This is said to represent St. Michael, the patron saint.

THE CHURCH AT CAUDEBEC.

PLATES LXIV. LXV.

The church at Caudebec, a town seated on the eastern bank of the river Seine, about eighteen miles north of Rouen, is an interesting specimen of that style of architecture in which the transition from fifteenth-century Flamboyant to sixteenth-century Renaissance is foreshadowed, as may be seen in the engraving, *Plate LXIV.* [The church being erected in the fifteenth and sixteenth centuries, was commenced in the Gothic, and terminated in the Renaissance style. It consists of nave and side aisles, with chapels, and a choir with radiating chapels. The greater portion of the church dates from 1450, and the architect, who died in 1484, lies buried in the church. The tower on the north side of the church was begun in 1426, and rises with its spire to a height of 320 feet, the flamboyant tracery in it taking the form of fleurs-de-lis.]

[1] This porch nearly resembles the southern porch to the church of St. Ouen at Rouen.

The engraving, *Plate LXIV.*, shows one compartment of the sacristy externally, also a section and details at large. The windows and ornaments of this part of the building are unlike anything we have in England, and seem to belong rather to the domestic than to the ecclesiastical architecture, as may be seen by referring to the engravings of Fontaine le Henri and the Hôtel de Bourgtheroulde, *Plates LXXI.—LXXIII.* and *LV. LVI.* In *Plate LXV.* there is given a plan and section of a part of the church, called the *Lady Chapel*, which was chosen for delineation on account of the singularly constructed pendantive roof.[1] Dr. Dibdin says, "The church has numerous side chapels and figures of patron saints. The entombment of Christ, in white marble, at the end of the Chapel of the

[1 An interesting correspondence relative to the section of this pendantive roof, *Plate LXV.*, appeared in the *Builder* in 1871, in consequence of some doubts having been expressed as to its exact correctness, from the difficulty of obtaining entrance to the hollow space or pocket between the upper and lower webs, and the explanations of Mr. Benjamin Ferrey and Mr. Talbot Bury, who accompanied Mr. Pugin and measured the whole chapel, are of considerable interest, not only placing beyond dispute the accuracy and correctness of the measured drawings, but showing the eager interest in mediæval art which Pugin was able to impart to others. Mr. Ferrey writes, p. 1042, vol. xxviii., "I have a most vivid recollection of the intense interest which the elder Pugin felt in the construction of the great pendant of this chapel. I can answer for it that there is nothing in his illustration of it as shown in *Plate LXV.* but what is perfectly correct. An opening being made through the tufa of the groining at the top, some of us got in, and no little trouble was it to get out again: but, with a light, there was no difficulty in ascertaining the sizes of the voussoirs resting upon the huge keystone of the groining, a monolith of upwards of seventeen feet long. There may be some conjecture as to the sizes of the voussoirs built into the external angular buttresses, but in all probability they would correspond with those visible to the eye. The striking feature, however, of the Lady Chapel, both in execution and effect, is this surprising pendant; its appearance looks quite perilous, and until Pugin, with his wonted energy, had a hole made and found out the exact nature of the construction, all sorts of notions were prevalent, many believing that iron suspension-rods, &c., were employed." Mr. Talbot Bury, in p. 20, vol. xxix., who measured the chapel, confirms Mr. Ferrey's statements, and writes, "I have a very vivid recollection of everything connected with the remarkable pendant of this chapel, and had additional cause for it, as, having got into a hole made in the inner arch, for the purpose of examining this pendant, I ran the risk of immolation for the cause of Gothic art, by a total inability for some time to get out again—thus nearly converting that very interesting groining into a very *uninteresting* mausoleum for myself. . . . I am able to take the responsibility on myself" (viz. of the correctness of the drawing), "as the plate of the Lady Chapel published in Pugin's *Architecture of Normandy* was drawn by me from my own sketches and measurements, in which there is but one omission, and that is—the junction of the large arch with the wall was filled in and weighted to hinder the upward thrust. The section of this groin in Gwilt, *Supplement to the Encyclopædia of Architecture* (published in 1851), does not fully explain its peculiarities, and would lead to the supposition that the whole of the top of the groining is three feet one inch in thickness, whereas there are only six large ribs of that size starting from the internal angles, meeting in the centre, and holding up this pendant stone of seventeen feet long, from which the moulded groinings

Virgin, is rather singular, inasmuch as the figure of Christ is ancient, and exceedingly fine in anatomical expression; but the usual surrounding figures are modern, and proportionally clumsy and inexpressive."[1]

THE ARCHBISHOP'S PALACE, ROUEN.

PLATE LXVI.

Of this once noted edifice our illustration is confined to elevations, and a series of plans and sections of two turrets, which are interesting specimens of ancient domestic architecture, and both are appropriated to stairs. The principal façade of this palace was built about the middle of the fifteenth century by the Cardinal d'Etouteville, and consisted of several apartments, surrounding a large square court. At one angle of this area is a spacious gateway, of rustic work, in the Tuscan style: this is connected with a staircase, which leads to a state-gallery. [This palace has lately been restored, as well as the two turrets above mentioned.]

CHURCH OF ST. MACLOU, ROUEN.

PLATE LXVII.

[This church, the third in importance among Rouen churches, was built on the foundations of a chapel dating from the commencement of

and ornament are suspended. Mr. Pugin's plate gives two sections, one showing how the spaces between these large ribs are arched in with tufa of six inches thick, and into this a small hole was made by which I got into the space, where by candle-light I could examine and measure it all. I must further state that a part of the high-jointed roof was taken off to allow of entrance to top of groining. Having explained how the examination was made, I must direct attention to the very bold and yet careful construction here carried out. To avoid any pressure on the moulded ribs of the interior of the chapel from the subsidence of the large arch, a space has been left between them, and this has had the desired effect, for the joints of the moulded groining were as perfect when I saw it as if the hand of the mason had just left it; and all glory to those of the mediæval men who designed so beautifully and built so well."]

[1] Dibdin (Rev. T. F.), *A Bibliographical, Antiquarian, &c., Tour*, vol. i. p. 210.

the thirteenth century, and several times burnt; though mainly built between the years 1432-79, it was not terminated till the beginning of the sixteenth century. Its western porch is certainly one of the finest and most elaborate of the fifteenth century; it occupies the whole of the western façade, and is especially interesting on account of the peculiar arrangement by which it accommodates itself to the surrounding streets. The two side porches are placed at slight angles with the central one, to afford, as it were, a more easy access to those who came from the right or left. We have noticed a similar arrangement in the Church of St. Vincent, but here the porch is not detached from the church, but forms its west façade, the side porches opening directly into the side aisles of the nave.] Within this church, near the western entrance, is the unique staircase, delineated in *Plate LXVII.*, which represents it in elevation, section, and by plans, whereby its general design and subordinate details[1] may be fully understood. It formerly conducted to the organ-loft. The elegant *carved doors* of this church were executed by Jean Goujon, the eminent sculptor." [Within the last twelve years a flêche has been added to the central tower. The design for it was taken from a model in cardboard of the fifteenth century, which may now be seen in the "Musée départemental d'Antiquités." To M. Barthélemy, the architect to the cathedral, was intrusted the construction of this flêche.]

WOODEN DOORS AT ROUEN AND CAEN.

PLATES LXVIII. LXIX.

[The framing of these doors is unfortunately not shown, so that we are able to deal with their decoration only. This, however, seems to follow the construction of the doors; in other words, the vertical lines representing piers and buttresses may be taken to represent the *stiles*, and the horizontal cills and string-courses the *rails* of the framing.

[1] Mr. Turner states, that it was constructed in 1512, and, according to common phraseology, by voluntary subscriptions, although the volunteers were bribed by the assurance of forty days' and one hundred days' indulgences.

Portions of the decorative work would seem to have been nailed on afterwards, the linen pattern and probably the tracery in the panels having been carved out of the solid. The earliest example is that from St. Peter's at Caen, *Plate LXIX.*, No. 2, which dates from the second half of the fourteenth century; the others are fine specimens of Flamboyant woodwork, the intersecting of the vertical and horizontal mouldings being very characteristic of the style.

The treatment of the linen pattern in the middle panels of the door from Notre Dame at Caen is more than usually naturalistic, and would go far to prove the truth of M. Viollet le Duc's argument (*Dictionnaire Renaissance*, vol. vi. page 360) that this ornament was derived from a custom in vogue previous to the fifteenth century of suspending skins and tapestry in the panels of furniture.]

CHURCH OF ST. JACQUES, DIEPPE.

PLATE LXX.

[This church stands on the south side of the "Grande Place" of Dieppe. The present building was commenced in 1250, on the remains of an ancient monastic establishment, and was dedicated to St. Jacques in 1282. The chapels, nineteen in number, were not completed till 1354. The tower at the south-west end dates from 1443, and much of the interior vaulting is intermixed with Renaissance work. The lady chapel, though very pure in design, is still one of the latest specimens of Gothic work, the bosses of the ribbed vaulting are elaborately carved, and the ribs have small pendants at their intersections; the windows of this lady chapel are acutely pointed, and have horizontal transoms, an unusual feature in French architecture.]

Of this very interesting edifice we have only one engraving, representing part of a very elaborate stone screen in the north transept, or "aisle of the choir;" it incloses a chantry chapel, which, like the lady chapel, exhibits a singular mixture of pointed forms with Renaissance features;

parts of it are said to resemble the tomb of Bishop Fox, at Winchester.[1]] The plate (*LXX*.) shows the two doorways of the screen with rich pierced tracery above; on one half of the drawing the setting out lines only are indicated. In Mr. Cotman's *Architectural Antiquities* are views of the western front of this church, and also the east end, both of which display a profusion of enriched sculpture, in crockets, finials, tracery, double flying buttresses, an elegant rose window, &c. At the south angle of the west front is a square tower, of handsome design, and highly decorated with ornaments.

CHÂTEAU FONTAINE-LE-HENRI.

PLATES LXXI.-LXXIII.

The château or mansion represented in these Plates is situated about eight miles north of Caen.

The view of the whole front (*Plate LXXI.*), and elevations of two of its windows, will fully elucidate the external features of this château: it appears to belong to several epochs; the most ancient part is that on the right, which may date from the end of the fifteenth or beginning of the sixteenth century. The left wing probably belongs to the time of Francis I., there being in fact a date of 1537 on one of the windows.

Speaking of this house, and of two others of similar character in Caen and Rouen, Mr. Turner remarks: "Specimens like these are curious in the history of the arts; they show the progress that architecture had made in Normandy at one of the most interesting periods in French history: they also show its relative state as respectively applied to civil and religious purposes."[2] "This château," says the same author, "is a noble building, and a characteristic specimen of the residences of the French noblesse during the latter part of the fifteenth century, at which period there is no doubt of its having been erected, although no records whatever are left upon the subject. Fontaine le Henri was then still in

[1] *Architectural Antiquities of Normandy*, vol. ii. p. 38.
[2] Cotman's *Architectural Antiquities of Normandy*, vol. i. p. 68.

the possession of the family of Harcourt, whose fortune and consequence might naturally be expected to give rise to a similar building. As compared with the mansions of the English nobility, this château may be advantageously viewed in conjunction with Longleat, in Wiltshire,[1] the noble seat of the Marquis of Bath. The erection of the latter was not commenced till the year 1567, thus leaving an interval of at least half a century between them; a period probably much the same as may be presumed from other documents to have intervened between the introduction of the Italian style of architecture in France and England. Longleat was built by John of Padua—Fontaine Henri was also the work of Transalpine architects—both of them bear decided marks of the nation to which they owe their origin; but in the English mansion the Italian features are more decidedly enounced, while in the French they are strikingly modified by the peculiarities of their adopted country; and this remark would apply generally to all the introductions of foreign styles into our country when compared with those in France." Most of the exterior surface of this building is covered with "medallions, scrolls, friezes, canopies, statues, and arabesques, in bas-relief, worked with extraordinary care and great beauty. Their style is that of the *loggia* of Raphael; or, to compare them with another Norman subject of the same era, of the sculptures upon the mausoleum raised to the Cardinal d'Amboise, in Rouen Cathedral."[2]

[In *Plates LXXII.* and *LXXIII.* are given details of the window on ground floor, and of the upper part of the tower. They are interesting as showing the utter decadence of the Flamboyant style previous to the introduction of the Renaissance. The repetition of the cold and senseless blank tracery above the window and in the friezes, string-courses, cornice, and balustrade of the upper portions of the tower, serve as the best apology that can be made for the introduction of the Renaissance; a comparison of these two details with the altar-pieces and vaulted ceilings of the chapels of St. Pierre, Caen, or the cathedral at Senlis, or again with the magnificent monument of the Cardinal d'Amboise in

---

[1] Figured and described in Britton's *Architectural Antiquities*, vol. ii. p. 105, &c.
[2] Turner's *Tour in Normandy*, vol. i. p. 157.

the Cathedral of Rouen before referred to, cannot fail to impress the student that the Gothic style had died out in France, and that the Renaissance, with its graceful and artistic detail, supplied that innate craving for beautiful forms which distinguishes nearly all the architecture of the period of Francis I.]

STRING-COURSES, PARAPETS, &c., FROM VARIOUS BUILDINGS.

PLATES LXXIV.—LXXVI.

[The ornamental details represented in these Plates are from the various buildings, of which fuller illustrations have been already given. Most of them must be taken as examples of the later and more decadent period of Gothic art in Normandy, and show how the dexterity of the French sculptors led them in the fifteenth and sometimes in the sixteenth century to too close an imitation of nature. Thus we see in an example from St. Ouen (No. 1, *Plate LXXIV.*), the vine and grapes conventionally arranged, it is true, but copied as faithfully as it was possible, far beyond, however, the proper limits of stone carving. This is the more conspicuous in a series of examples in *Plate LXXVI.*, where the oak, the thistle, and other plants are all portrayed with extreme exactness. Nos. 3, 4, 2, 6, in *Plate LXXIV.* represent string-courses, in which the vegetable forms are properly conventionalized, and these are the examples to which we would call more particularly the student's notice, as exemplifying that treatment which is equally in accordance with the principles of nature and the materialistic properties of stone. The sunken quatrefoils underneath the string-courses of the Bayeux example is found also in the nave of the same cathedral. Another example exists in the upper part of the tower of St. Peter's Church, Caen. Three of the examples in these Plates are taken from secular buildings; they are all geometrical in their ornamental details, and the latter two particularly are essentially secular in their character.

Of the four types of balustrades and parapets given in *Plate LXXV*, three belong to the Flamboyant period, and are amongst the finest specimens in Normandy. The decoration in the string-courses, above and below them, are other specimens of naturalistic foliage.

The fourth example, from the Cathedral of Bayeux, is earlier and much more severe in style, though without the grace and beautiful flow of line which distinguishes the Flamboyant examples.]

SPECIMENS OF STAINED GLASS.

PLATES LXXVII. LXXVIII.

[As announced in the prospectus the coloured Plates of these examples have been omitted in the present edition, being calculated rather to mislead students than to assist them, from the difficulty of obtaining the actual tones of colour in the original glass.

The immense progress in the manufacture of stained glass which has taken place in England during the last thirty years, and the numerous works which have appeared illustrating old work has somewhat set aside the value which these Plates possessed, at a time when the revival of the manufacture by the second Pugin for various churches, and more especially for the Houses of Parliament, had not been thought of, so that these two Plates must rather be taken as suggestive of various methods of leading up glass than as models to be copied.]

THE END.

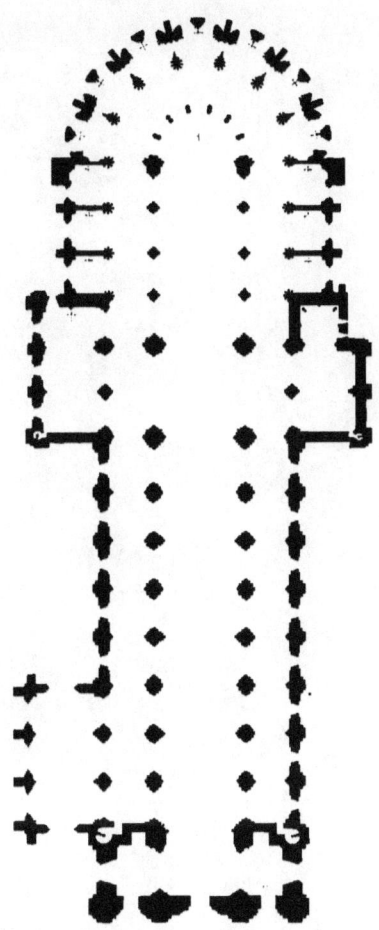

CHURCH ABBAYE AUX HOMMES CAEN

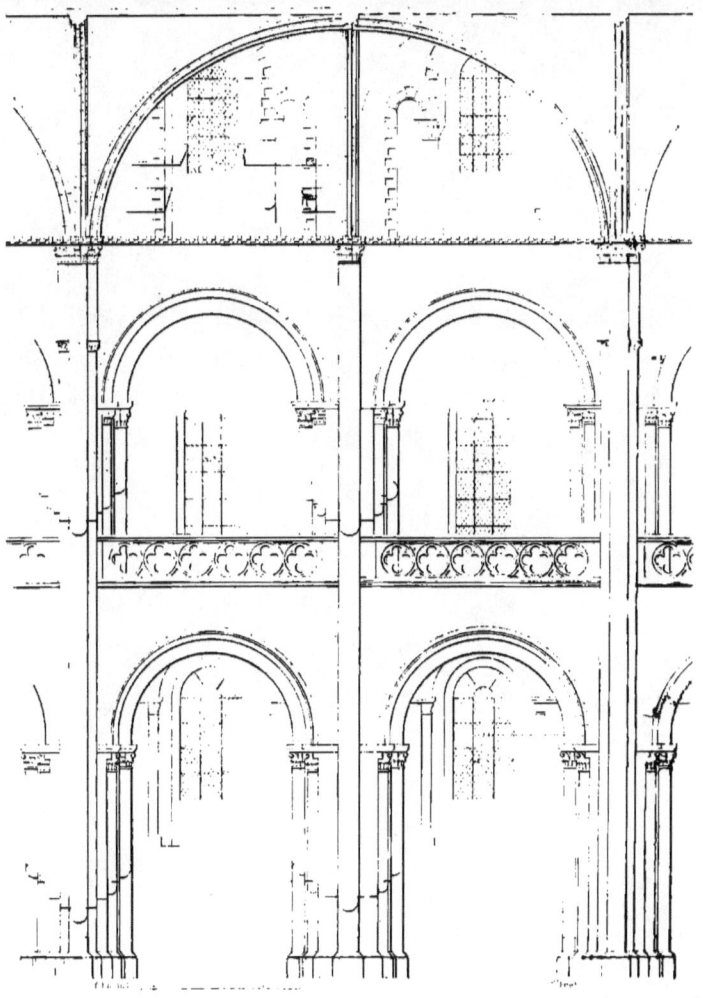

CHURCH L'ABBAYE AUX HOMMES, CAEN

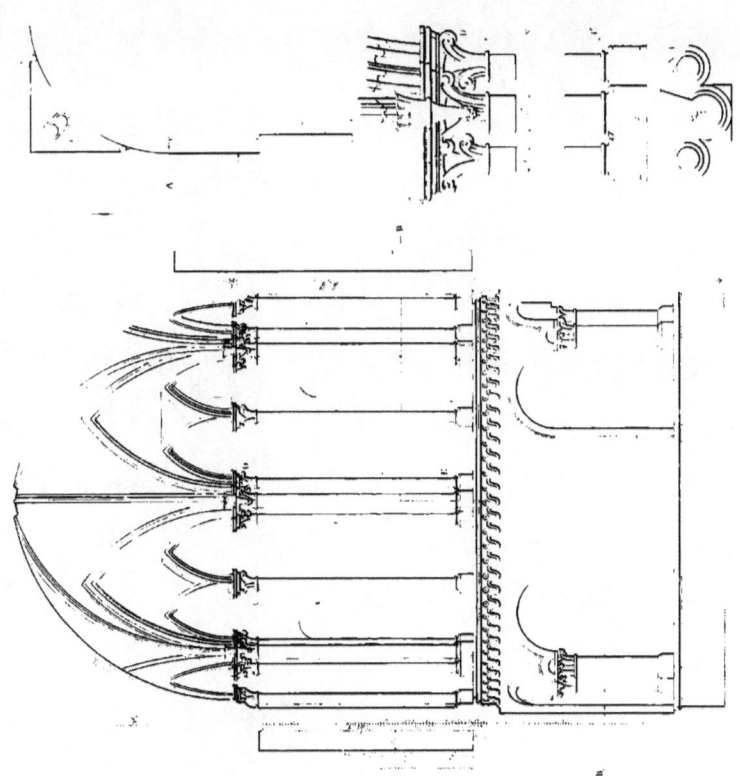

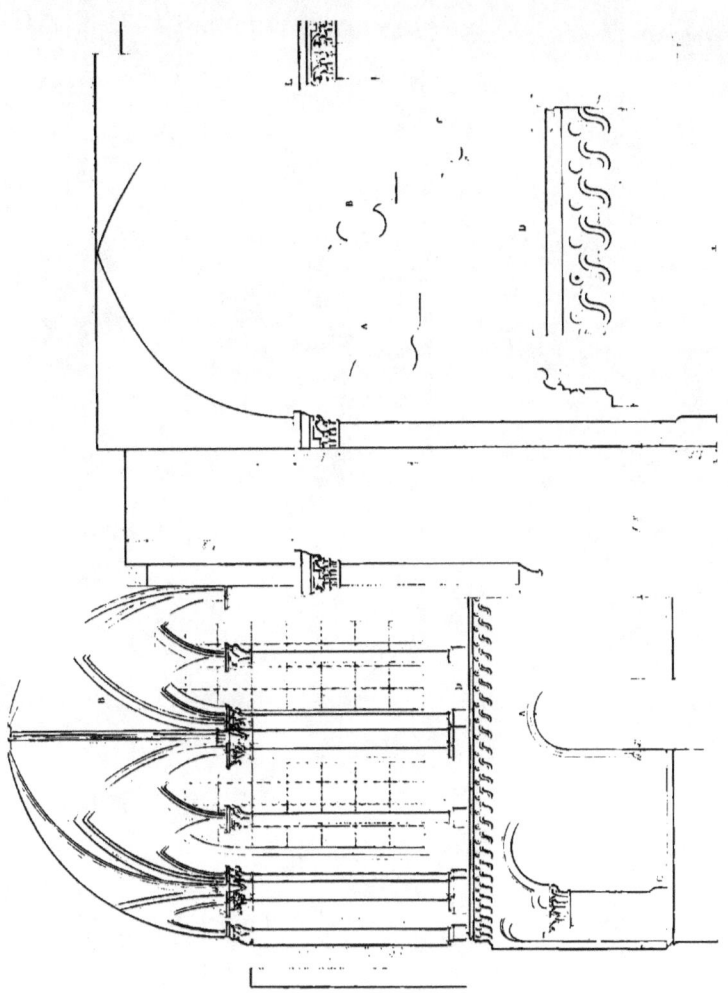

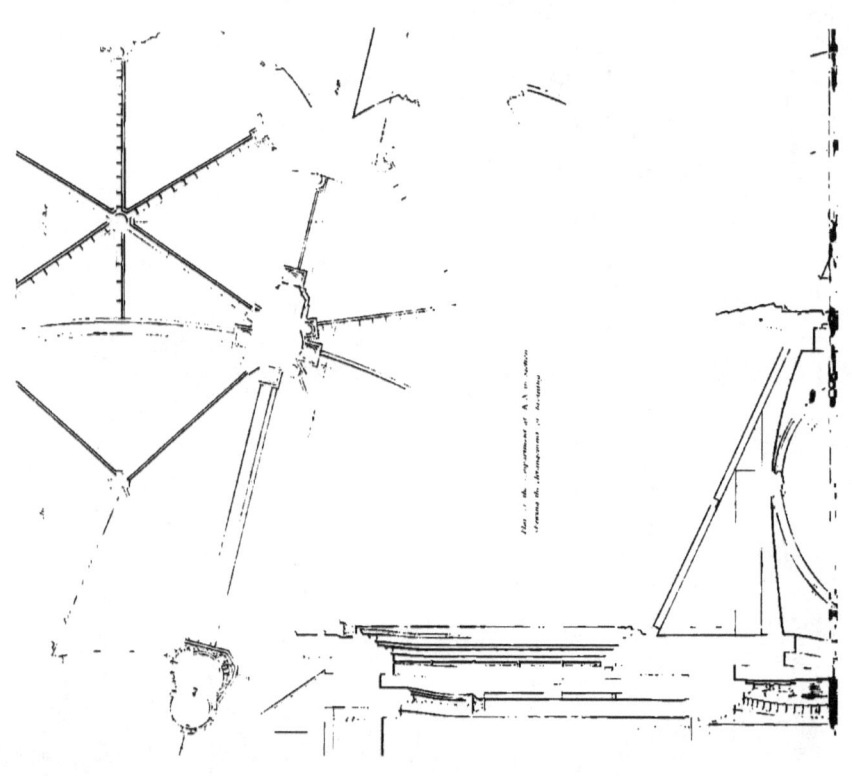

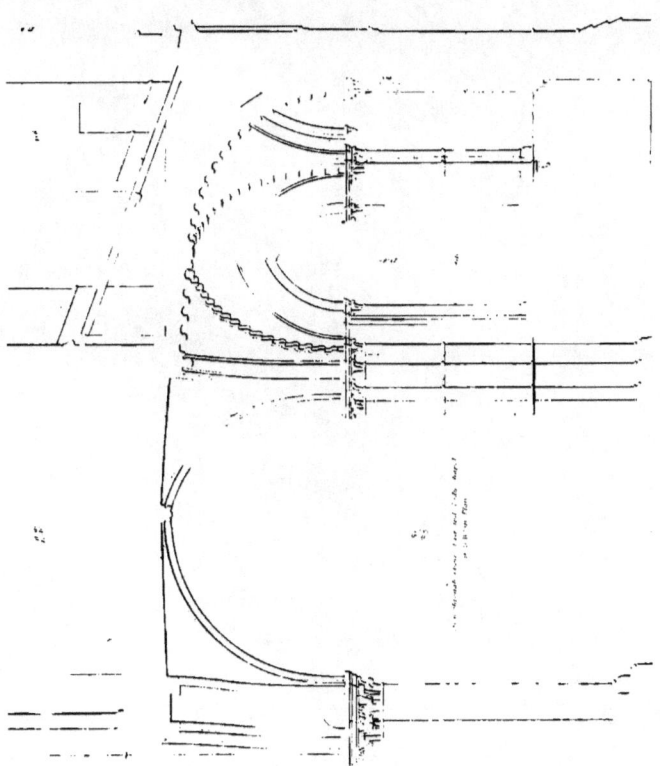

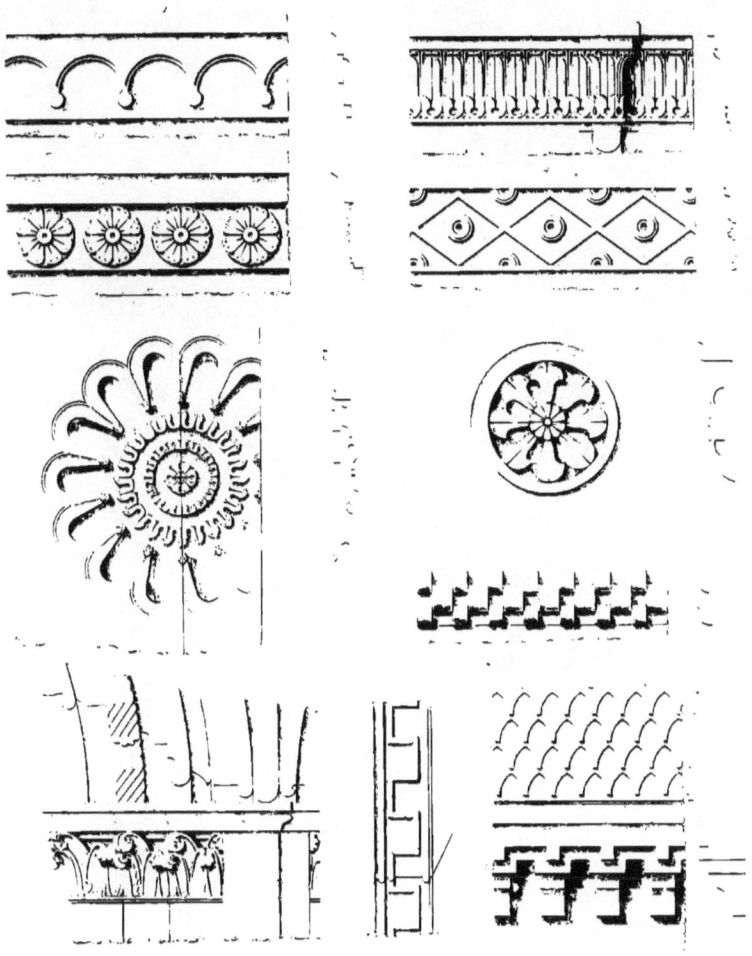

CHURCH OF ABBAYE AUX HOMMES
CAEN

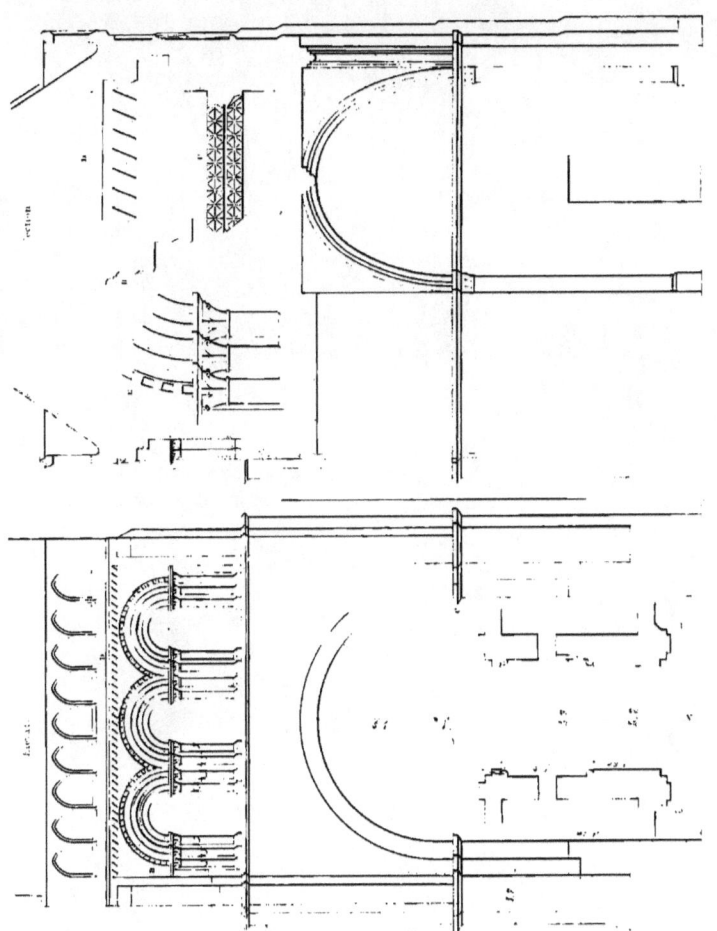

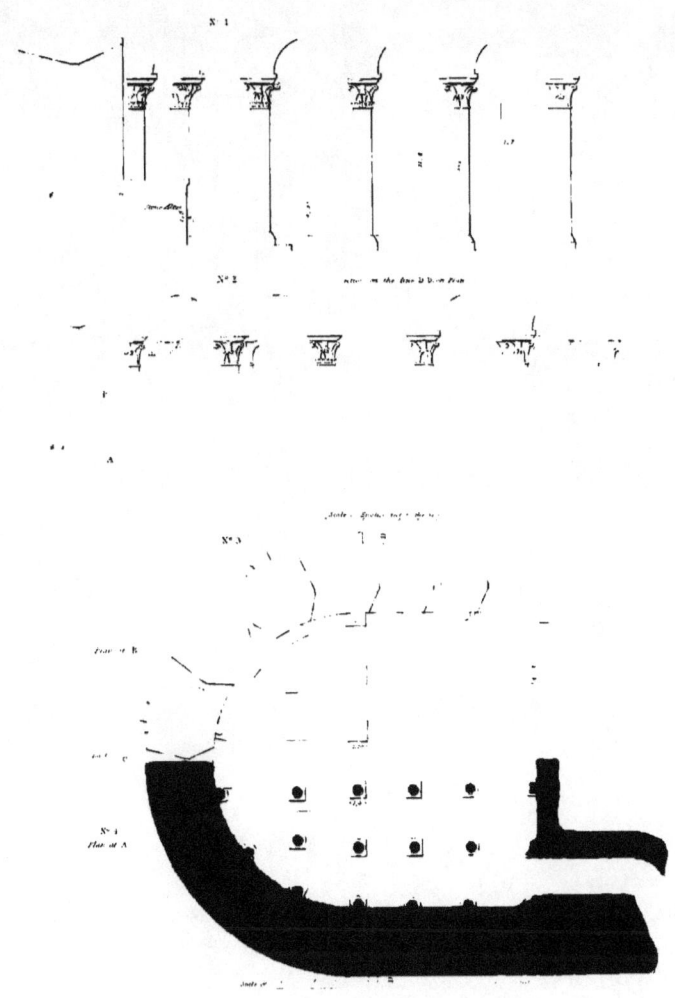

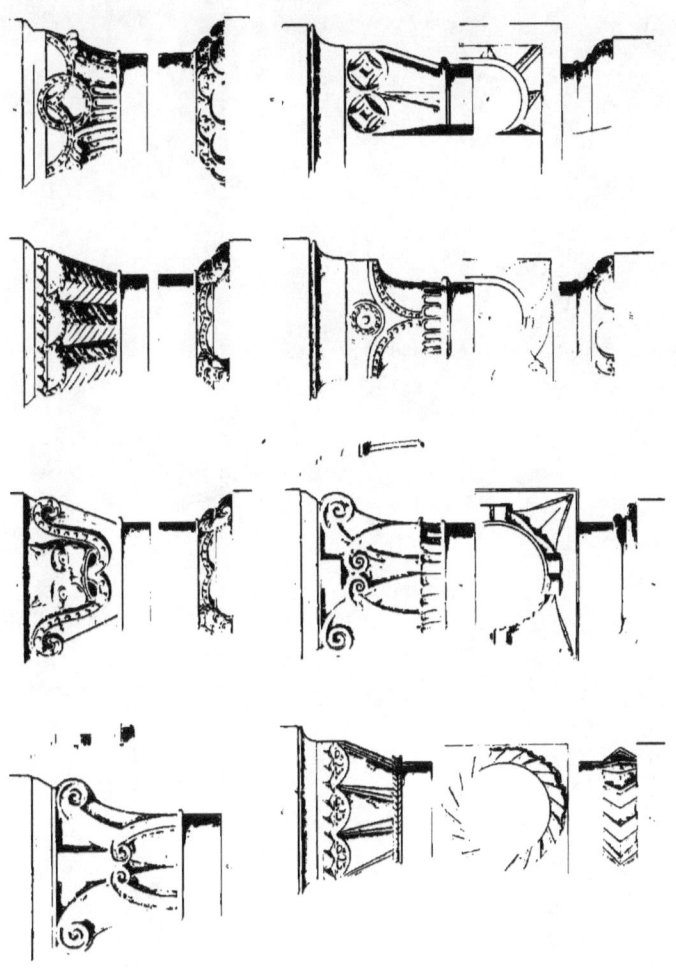

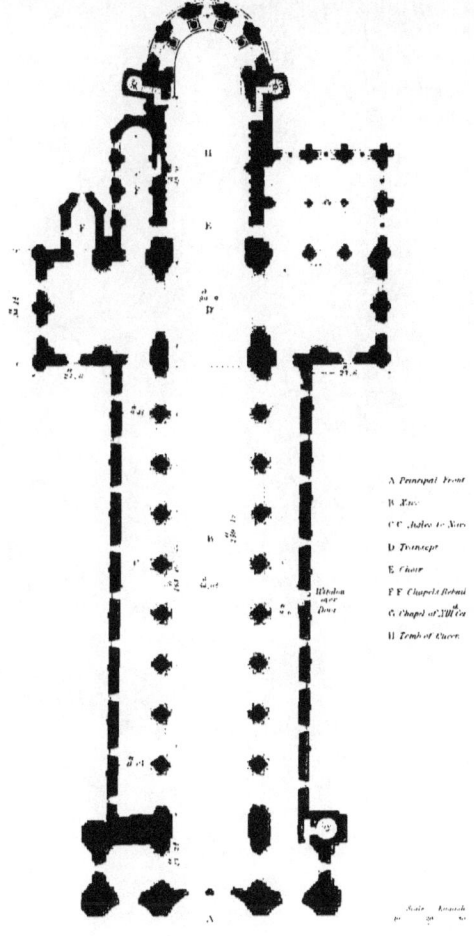

Ground Plan, Church of St Trinité
ABBAYE AUX DAMES
CAEN

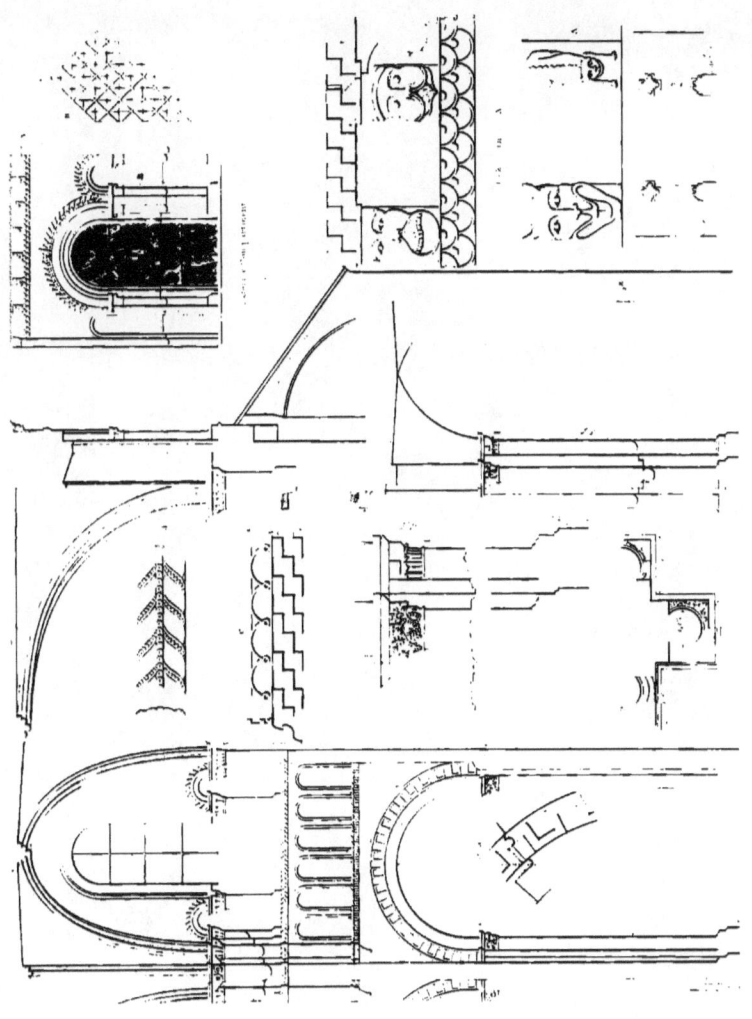

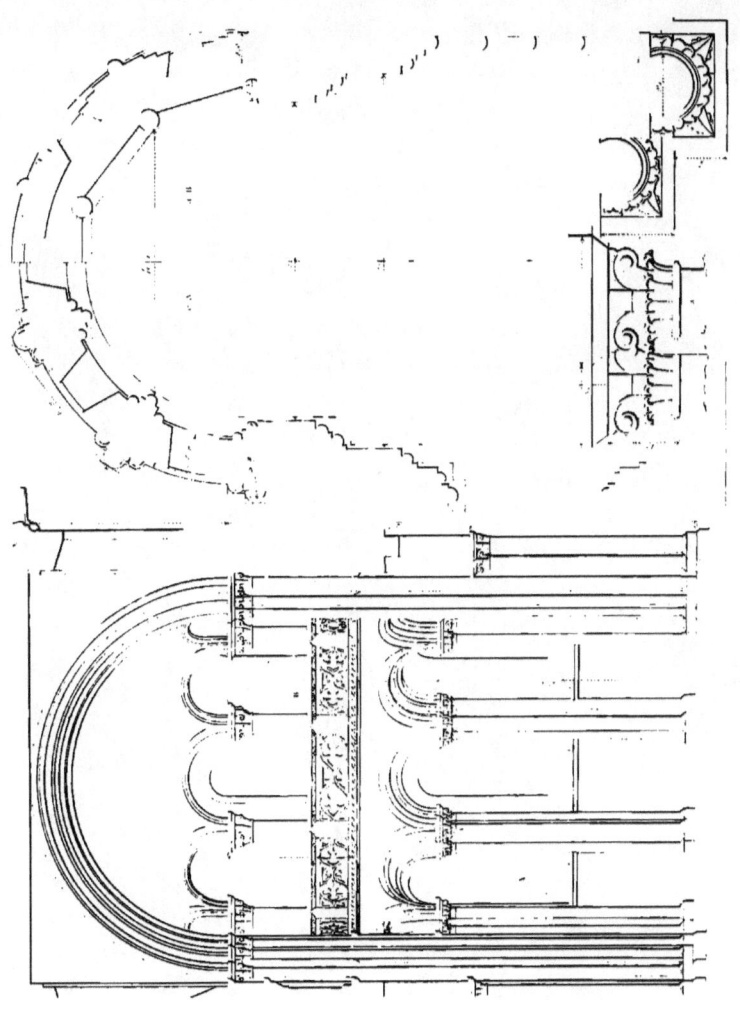

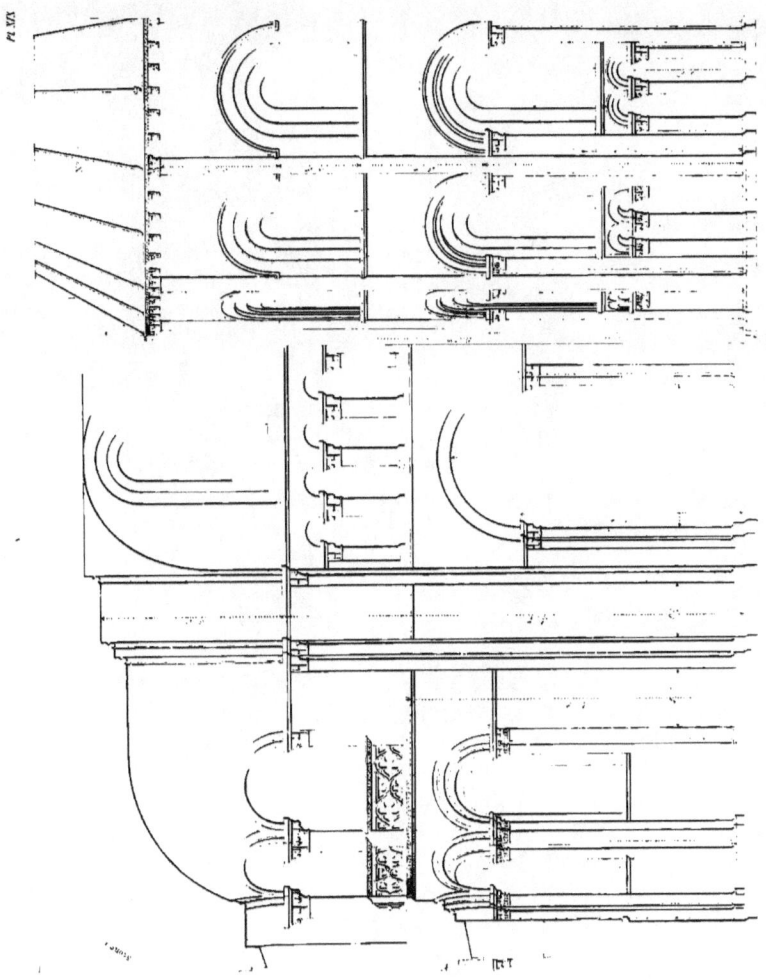

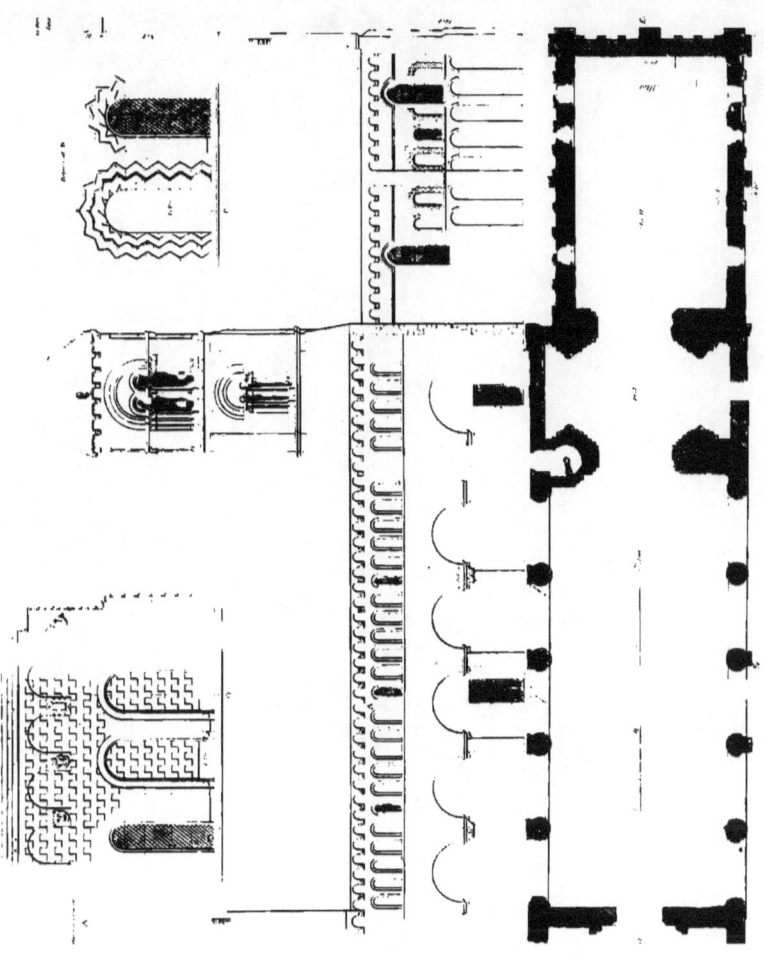

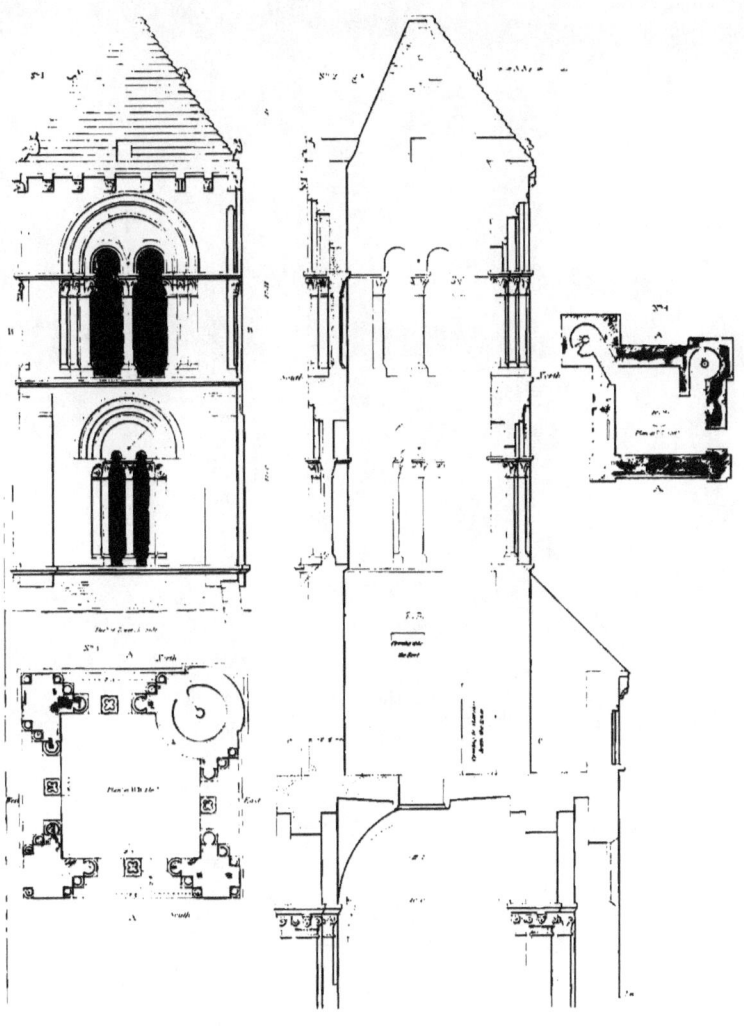

TOWER TO THE CHURCH OF ST LOUP BAYEUX
ELEVATION WINDOWS & CORNICE

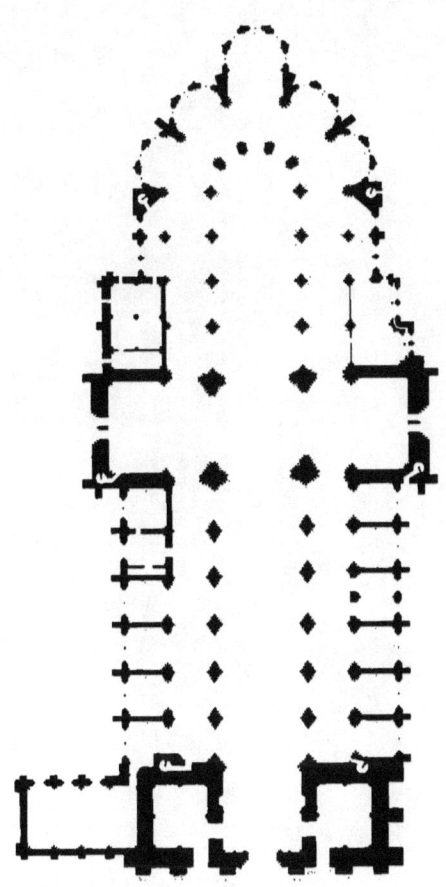

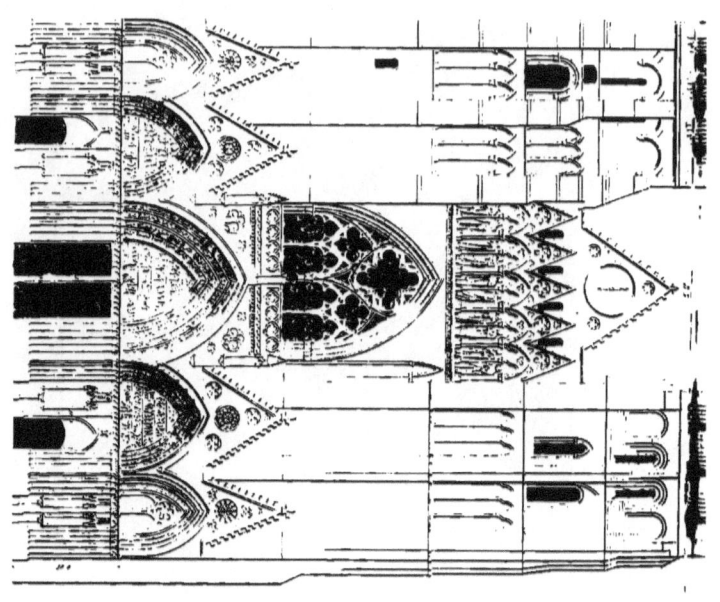

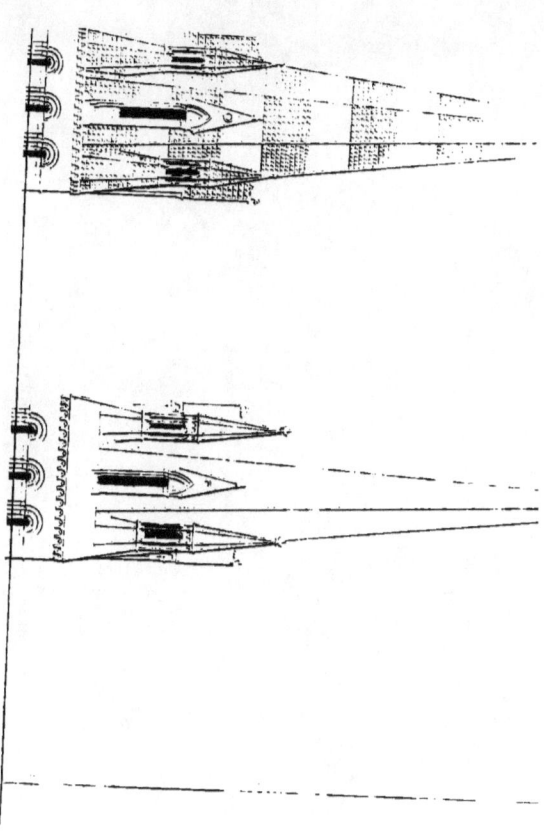

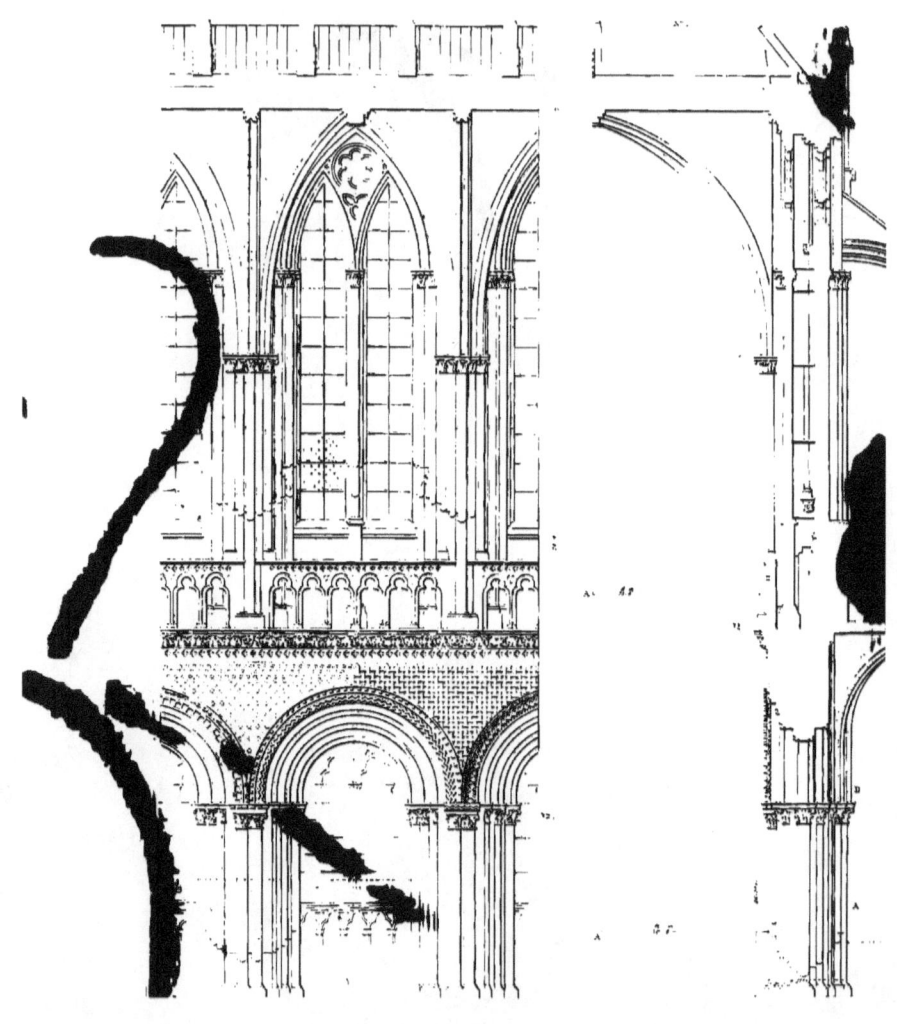

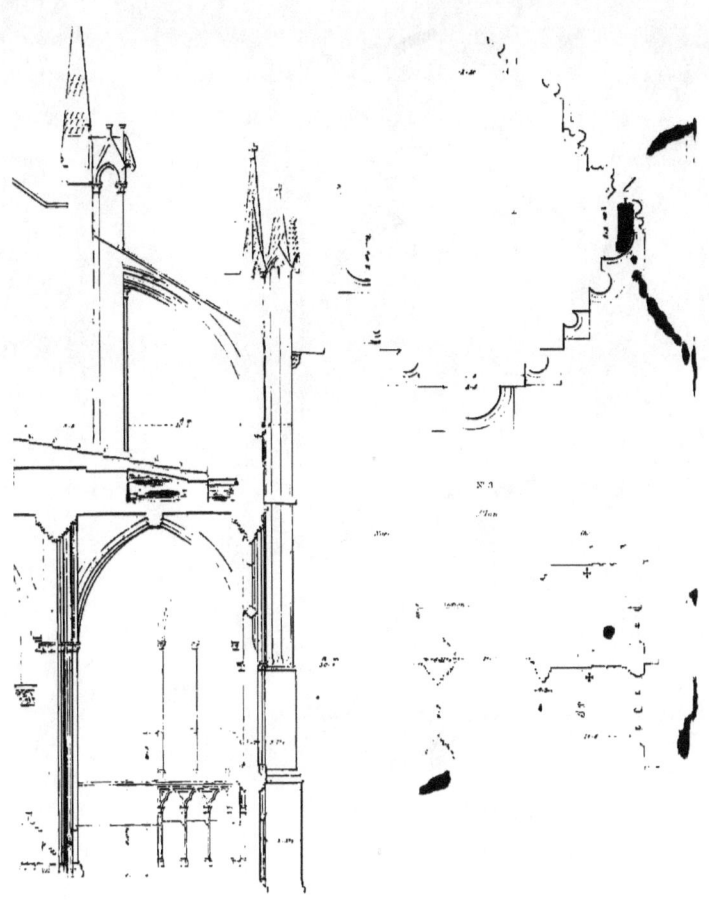

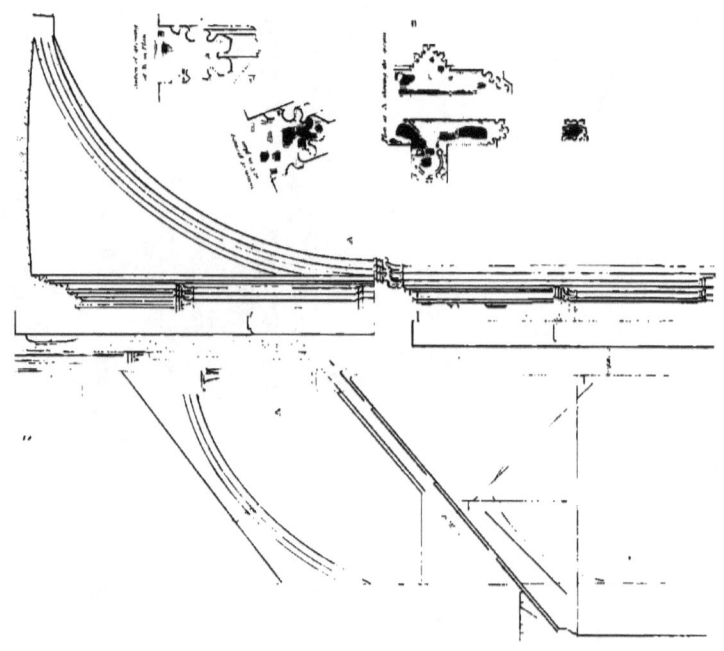

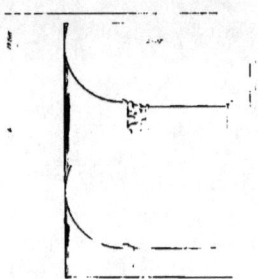

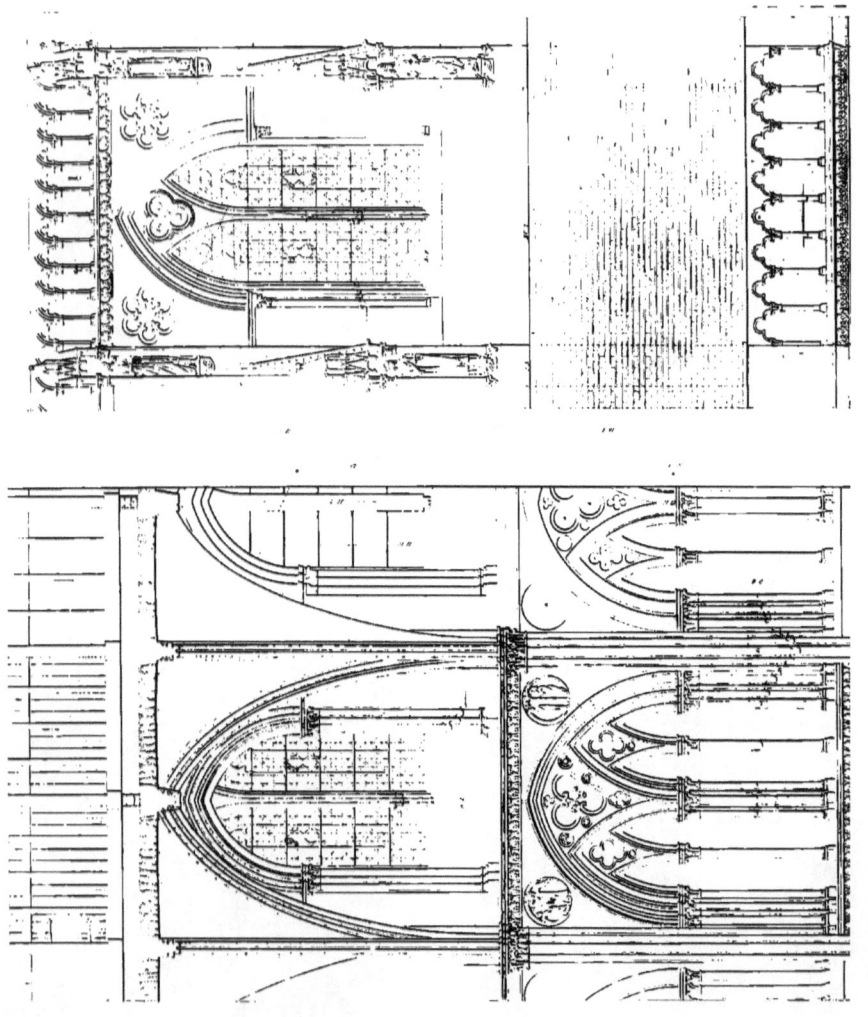

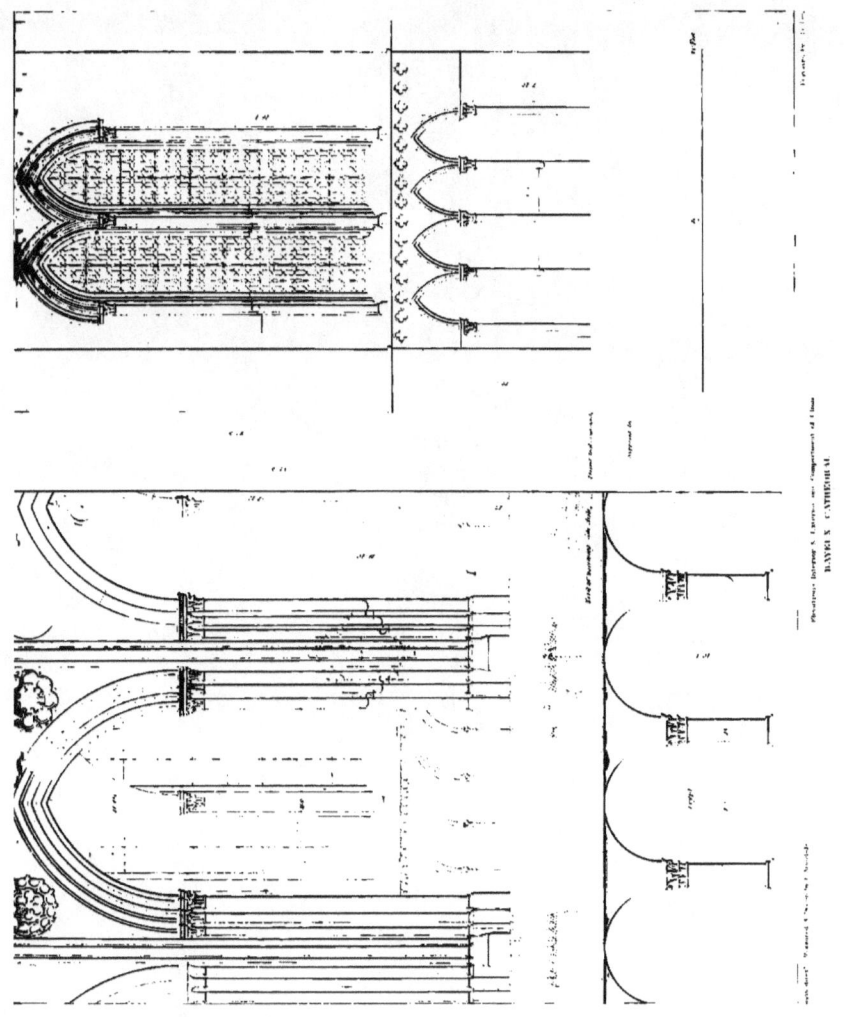

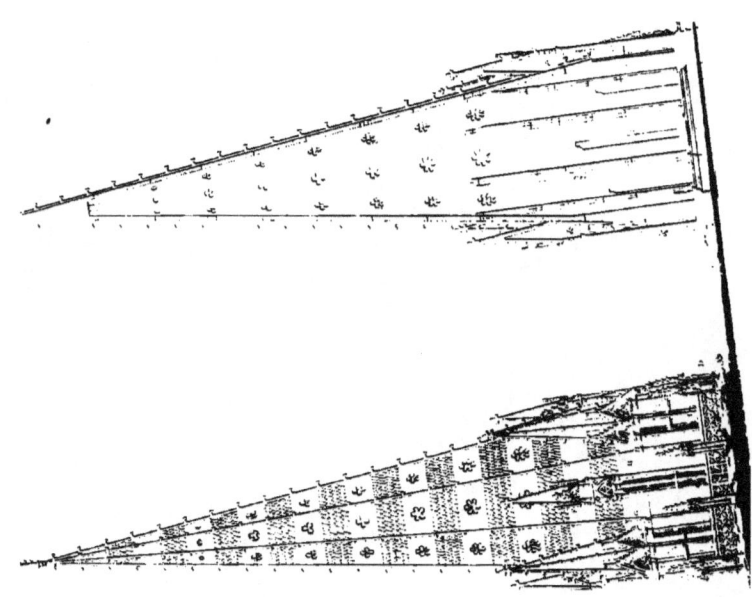

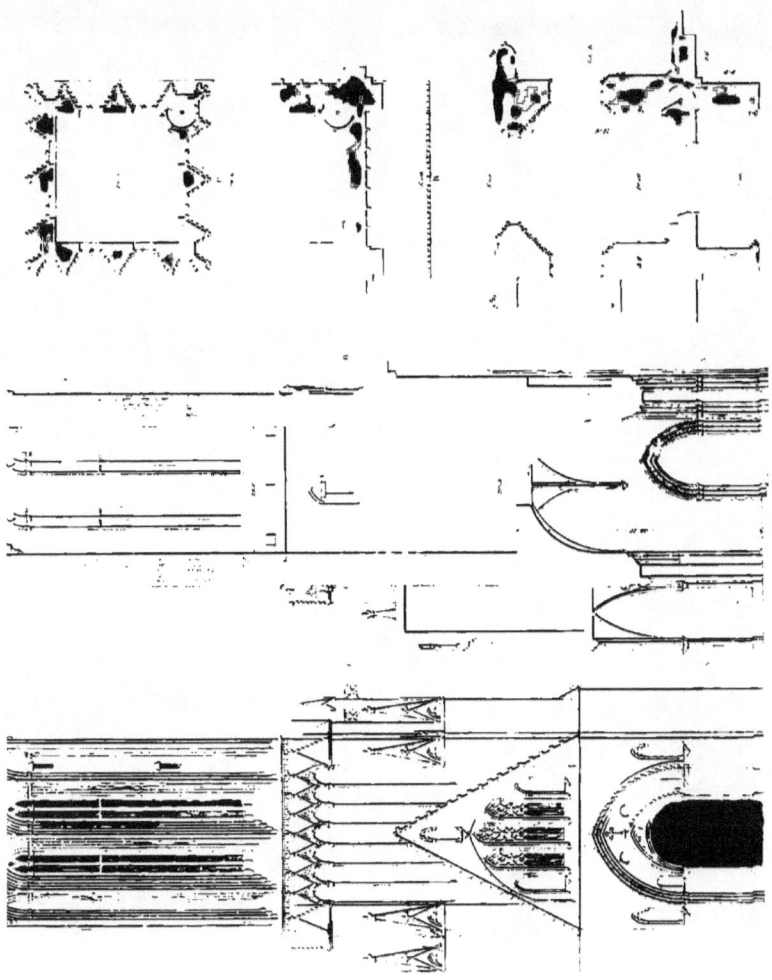

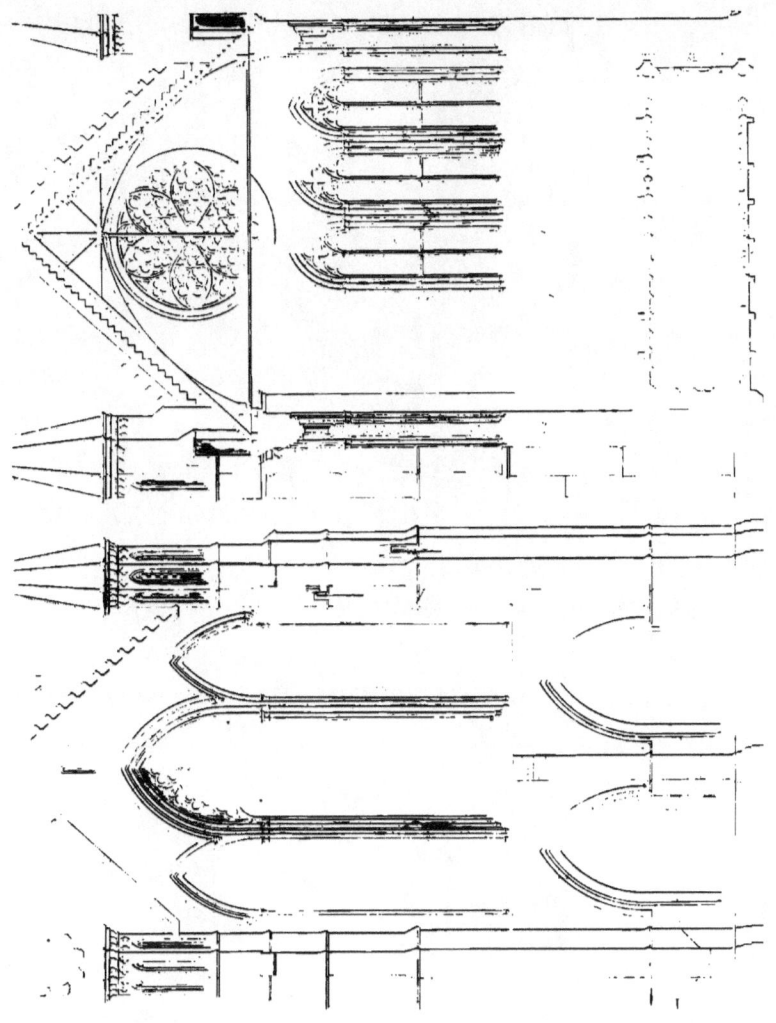

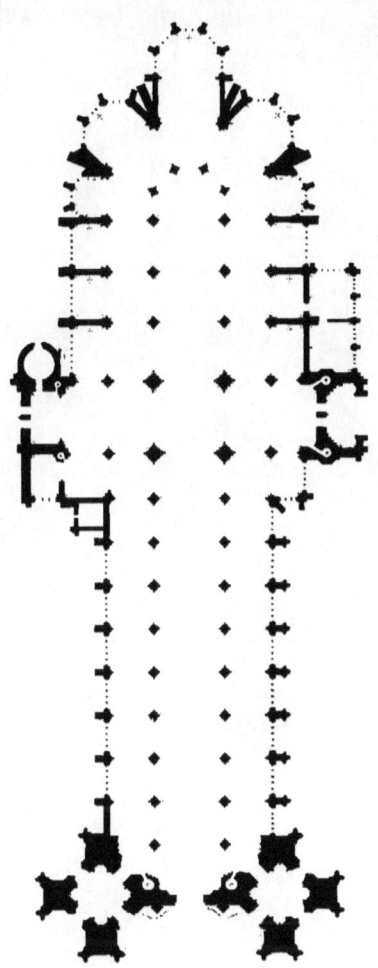

ROUEN

CHURCH OF ST OUEN, ROUEN

CHURCH OF ST. OUEN, ROUEN

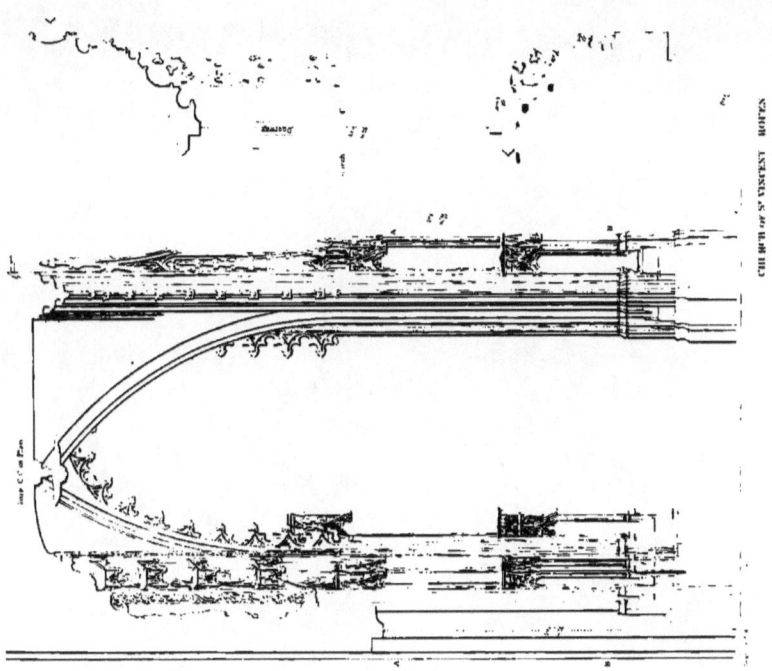

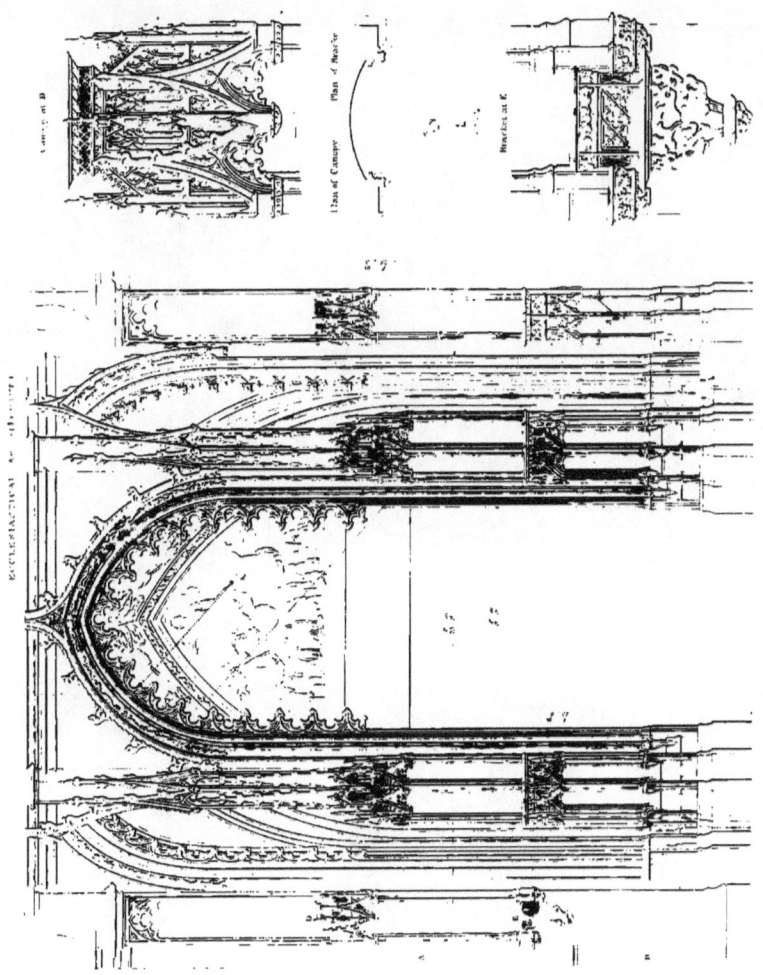

ROUEN.

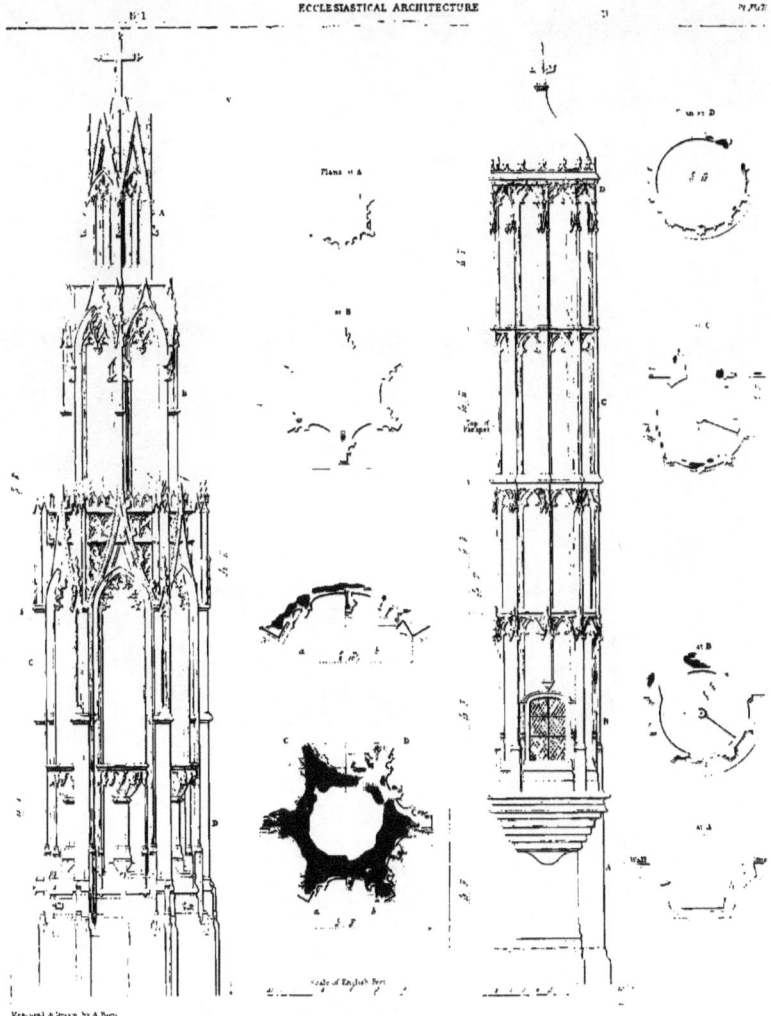

STONE CROSS & TURRET AT ROUEN

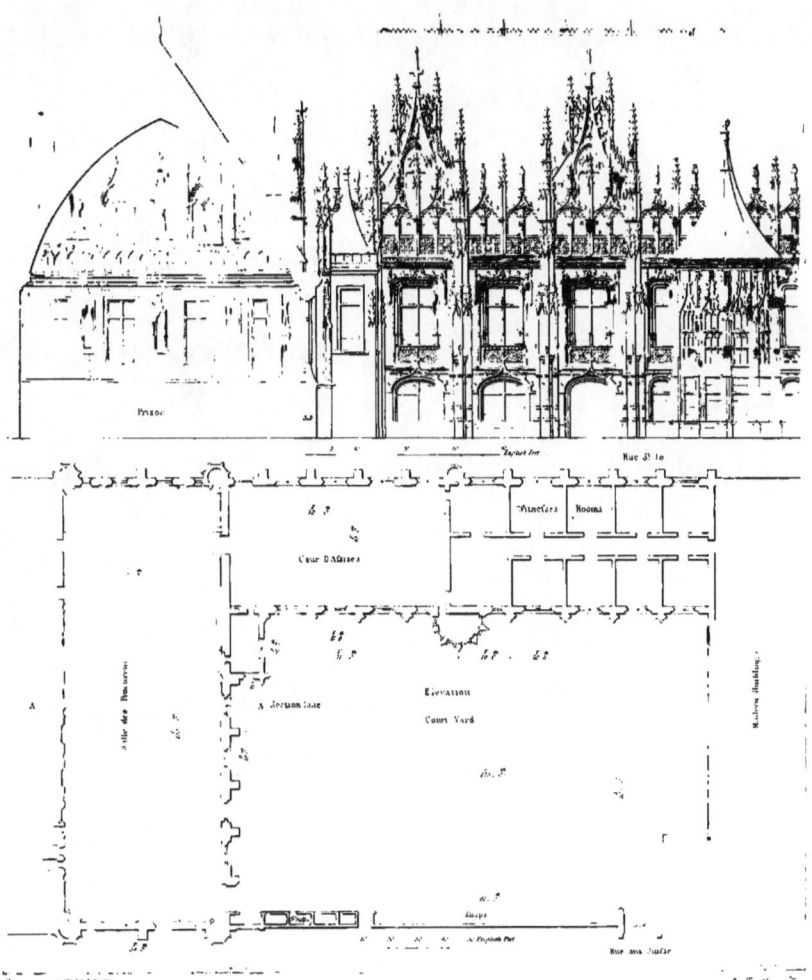

PALAIS DE JUSTICE, ROUEN.

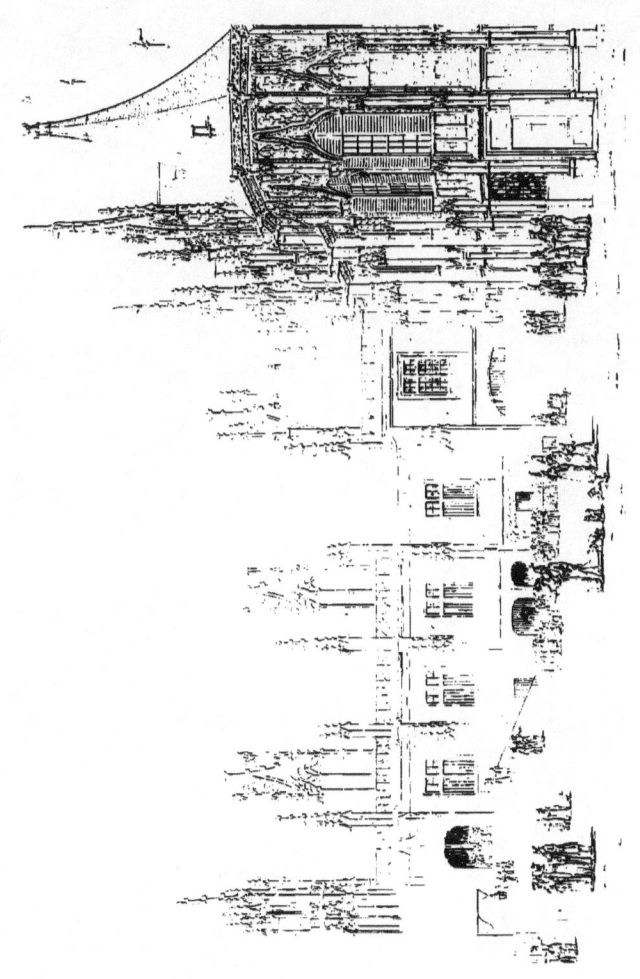

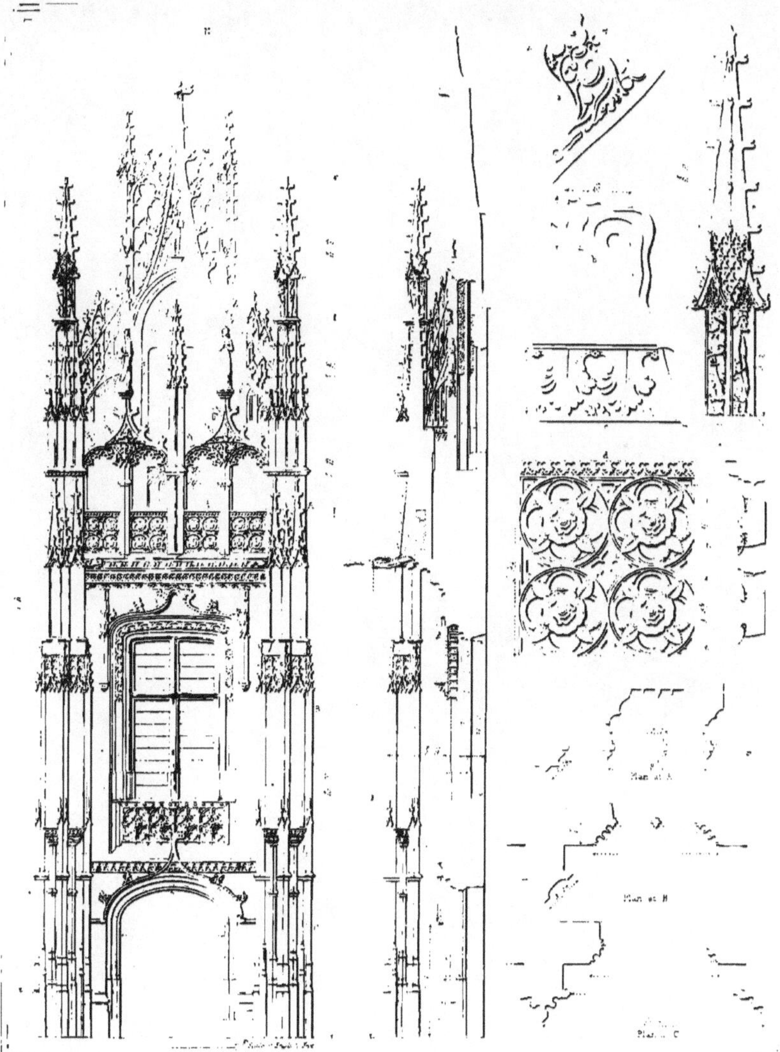
Plan at A
Plan at B
Plan at C

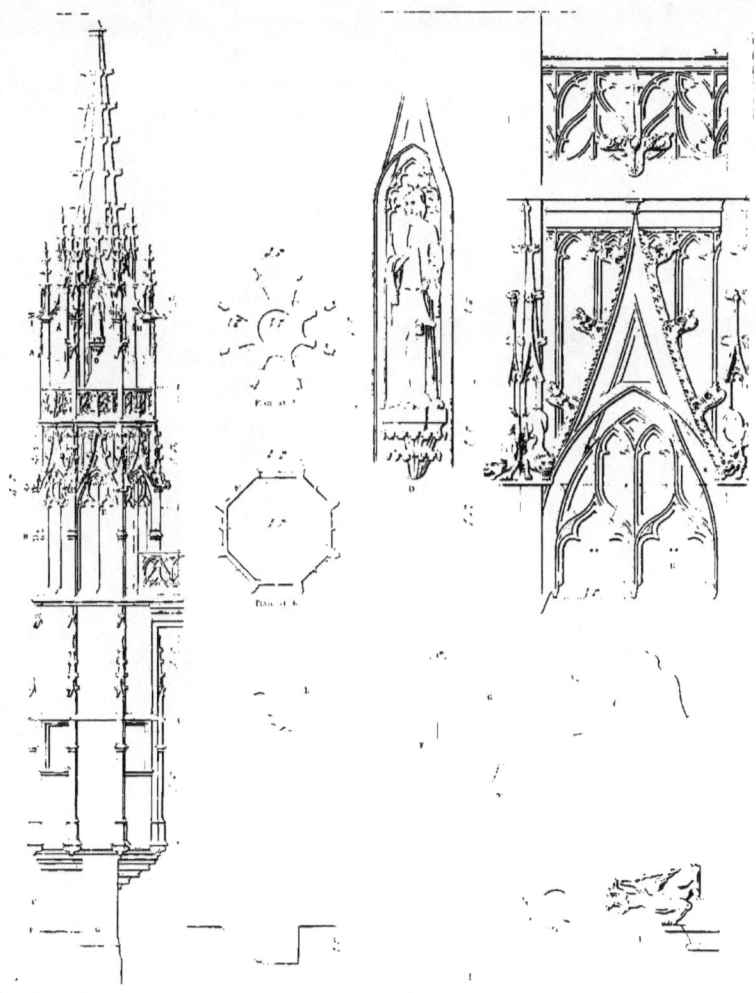

PALAIS DE JUSTICE ROUEN

PALAIS DE JUSTICE ROUEN

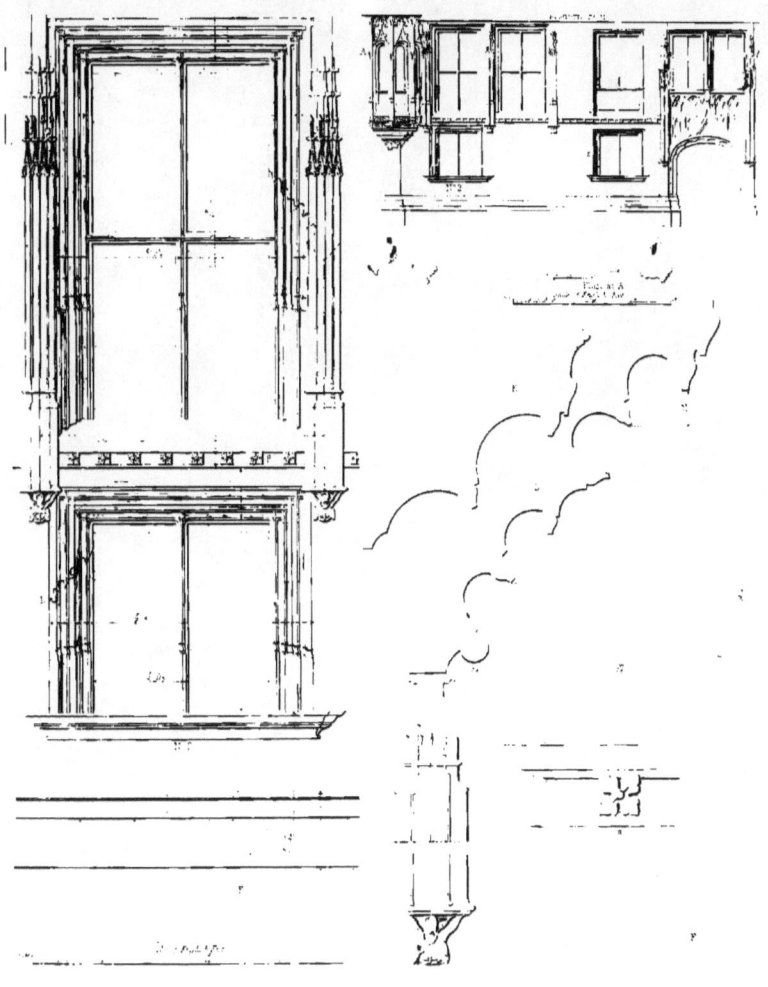

HOTEL DE BOURGTHEROULDE PLACE DE LA PUCELLE D'ORLEANS, ROUEN

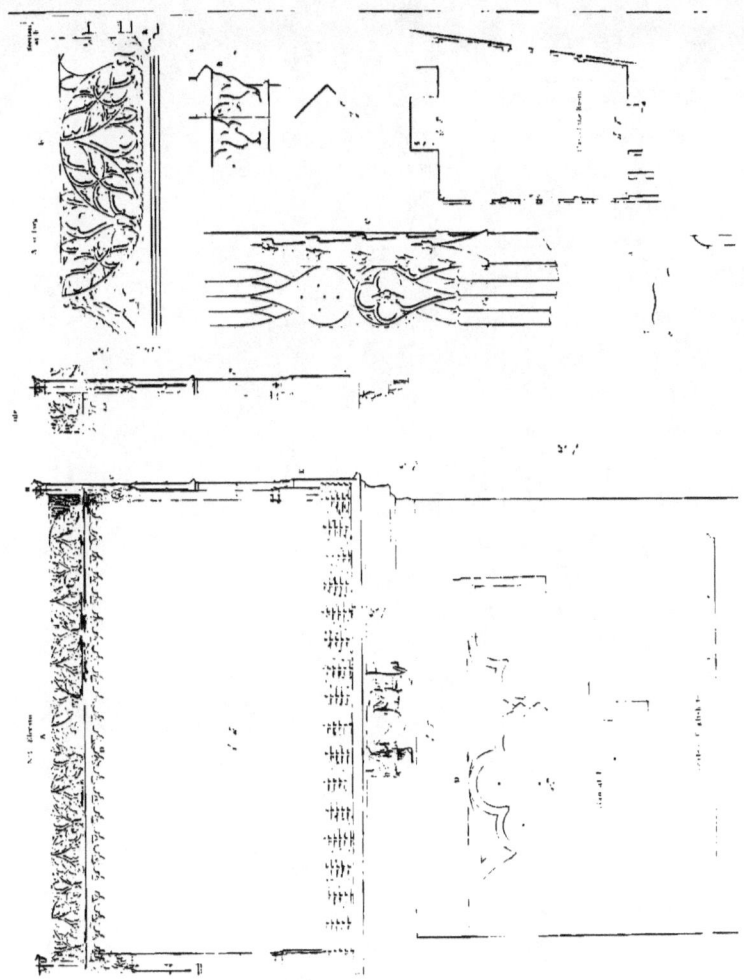

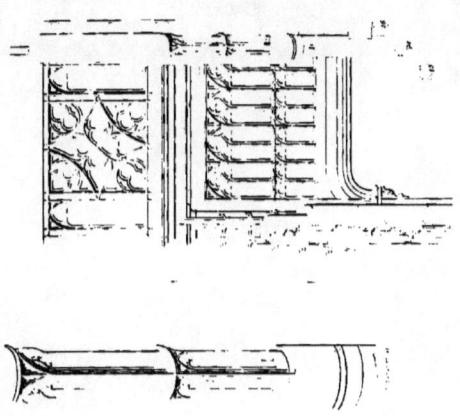

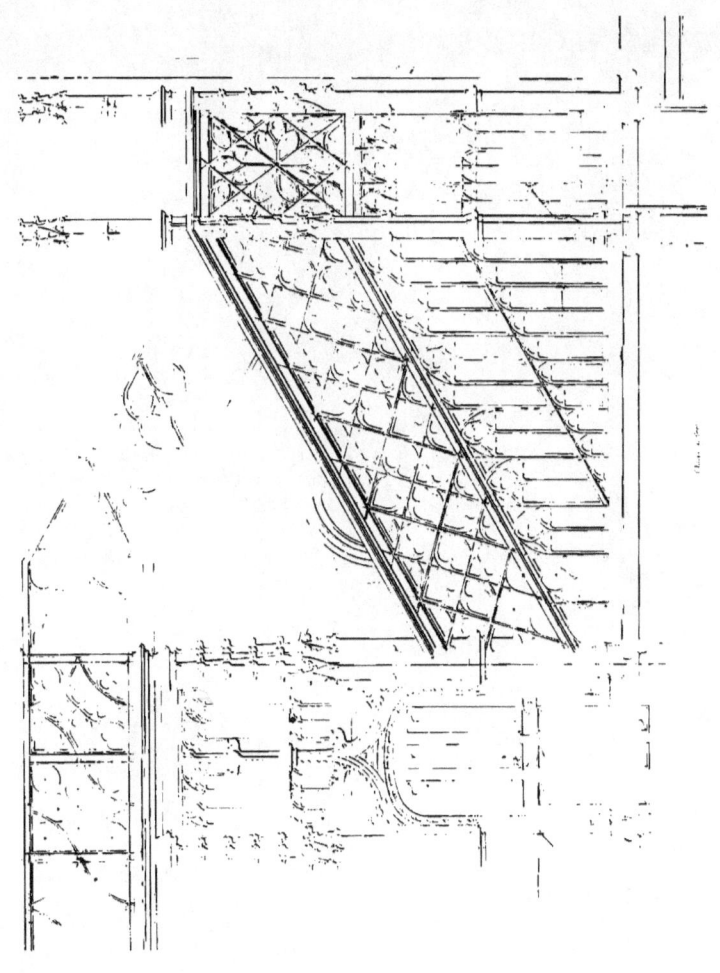

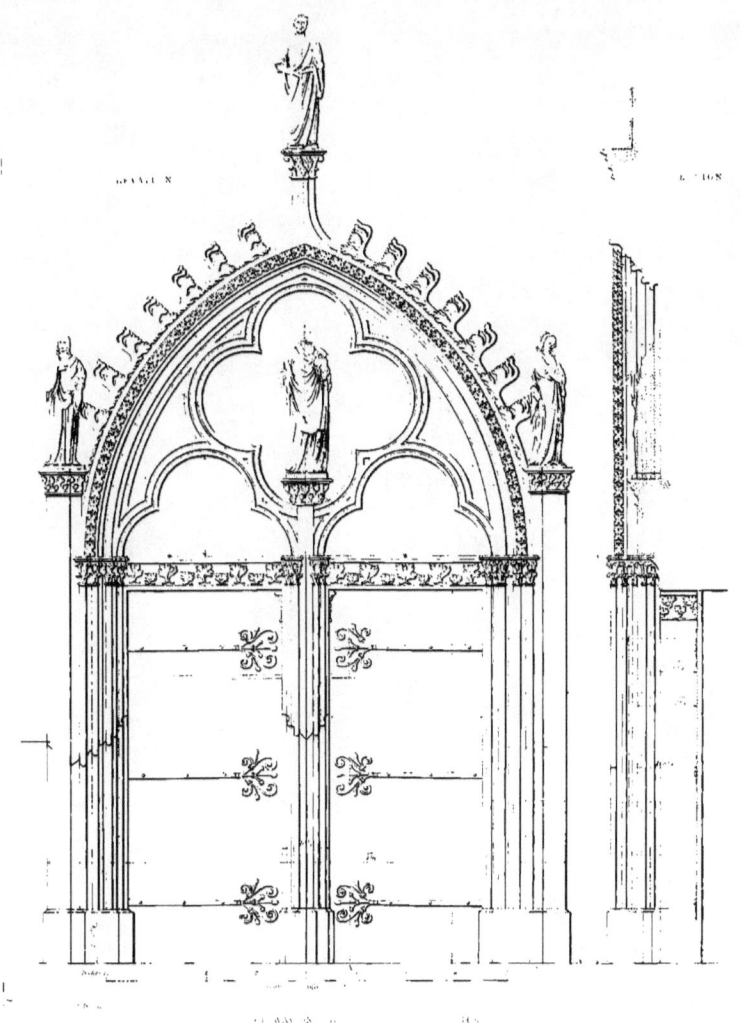

CATHEDRAL OF NOTRE DAME ROUEN

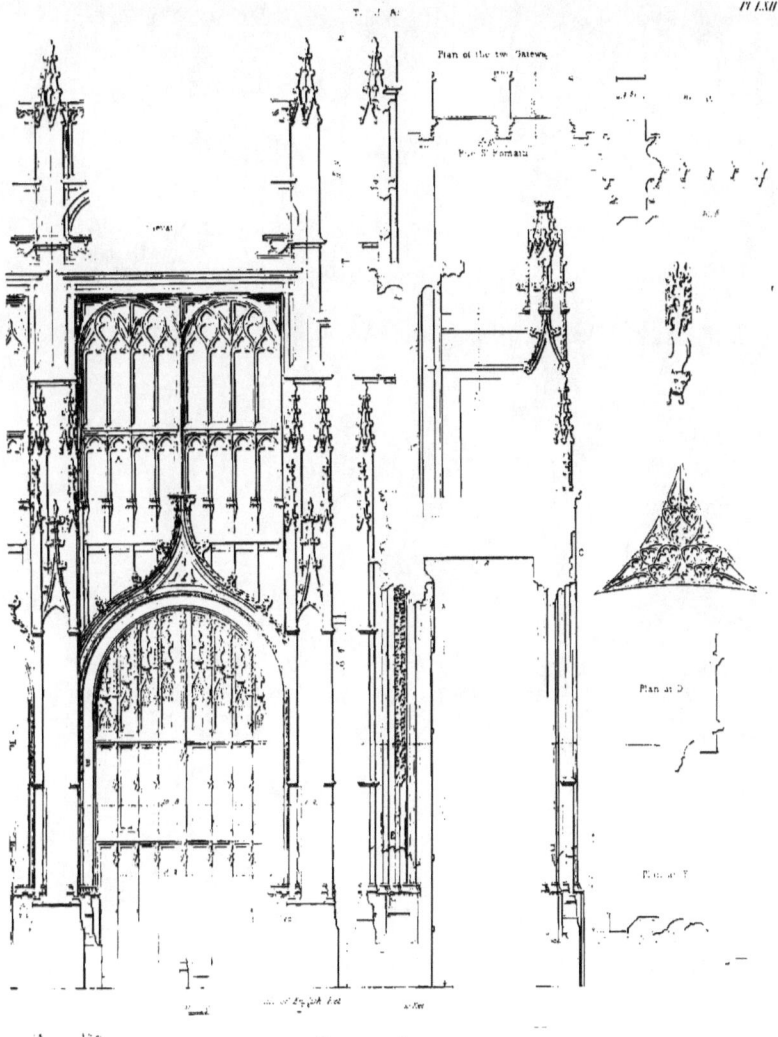

GATEWAY TO THE COURS DES LIBRAIRES CATHEDRAL ROUEN

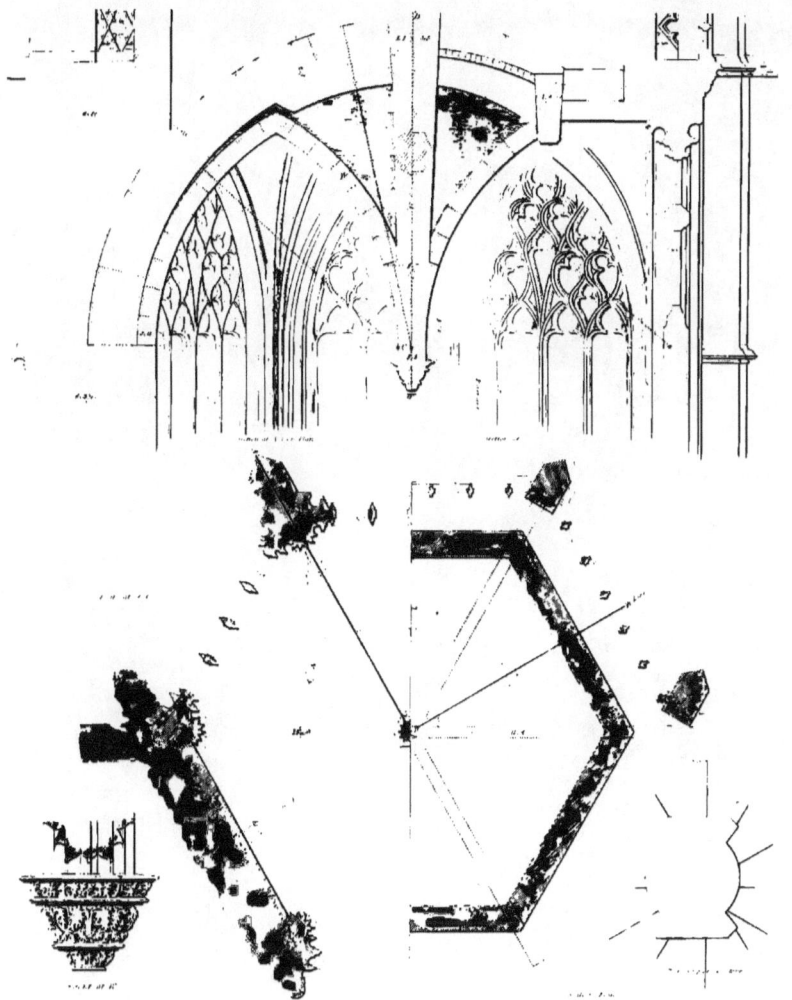

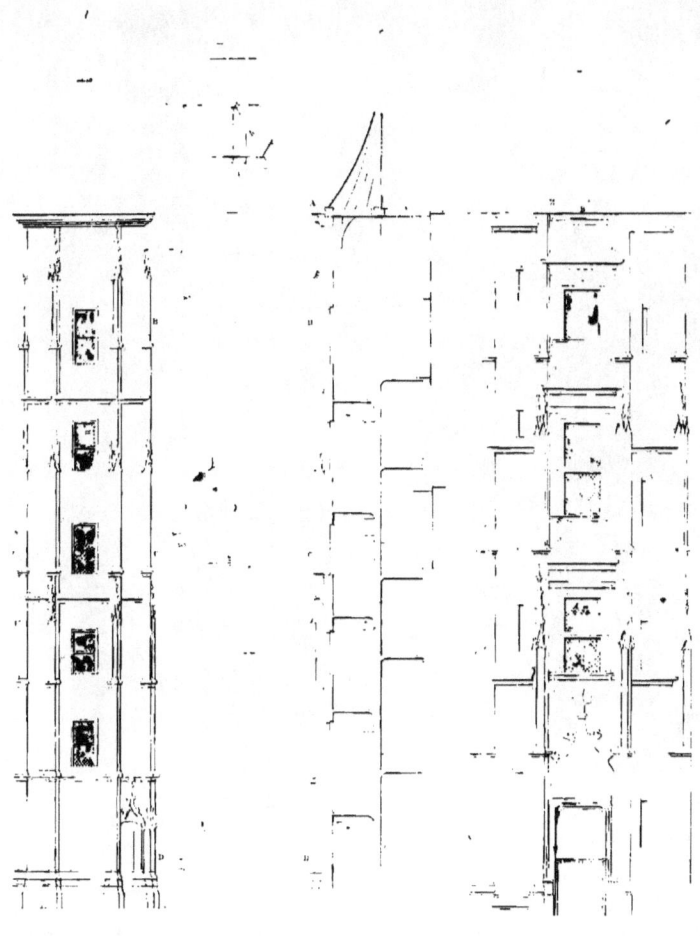

STONE STAIRCASE TO ORGAN LOFT — S.¹ MACLOU CHURCH, ROUEN

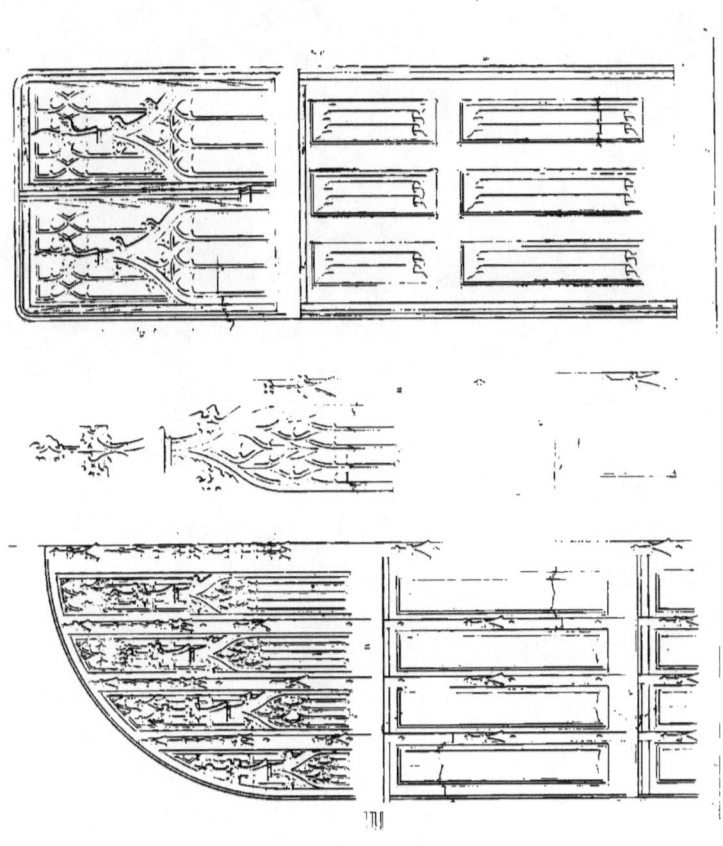

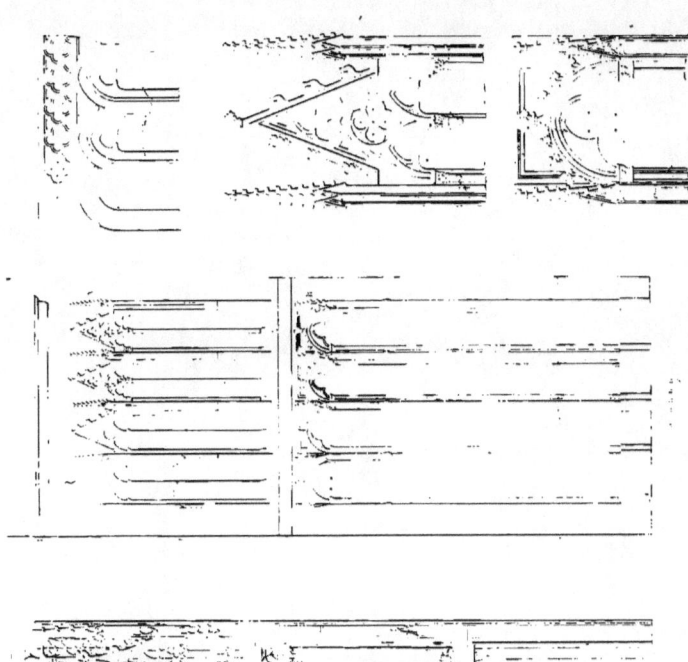

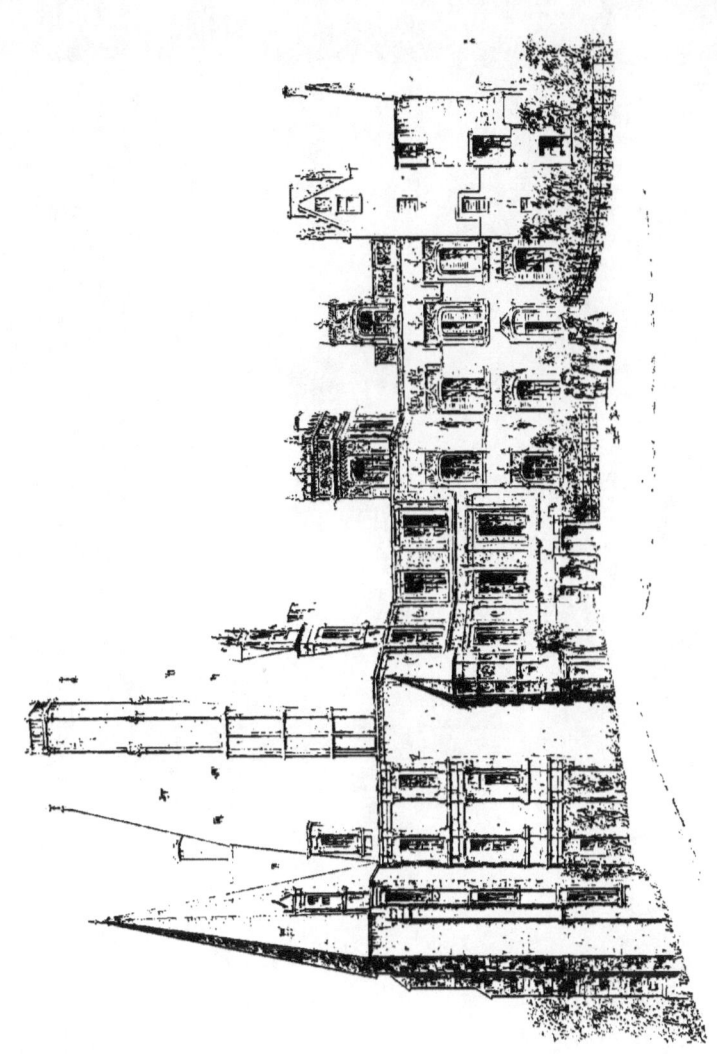

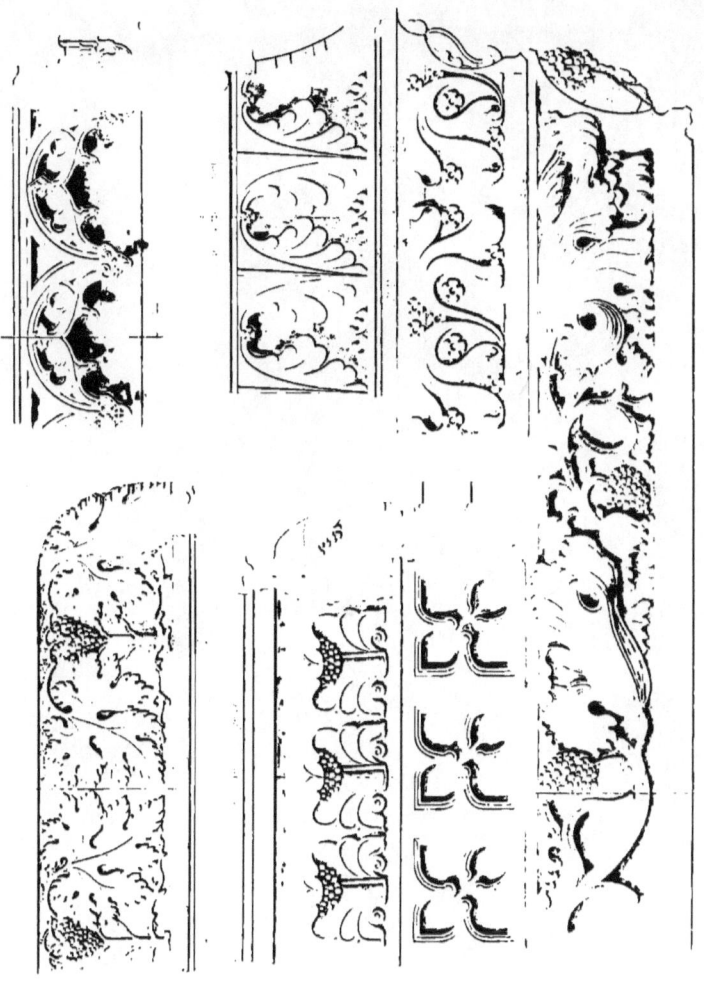

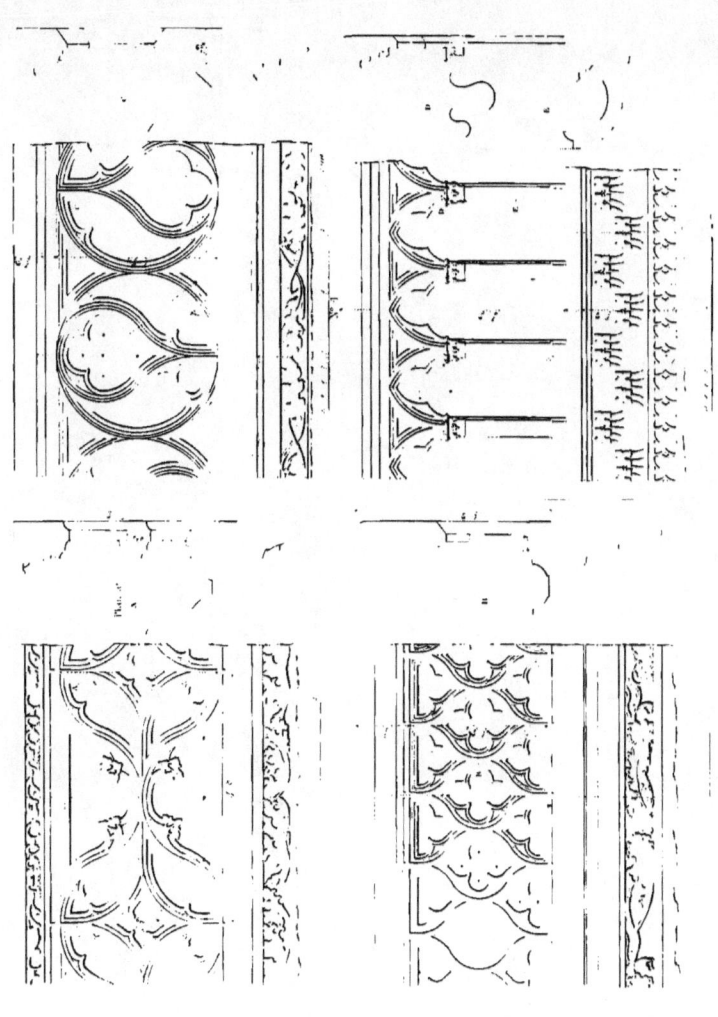

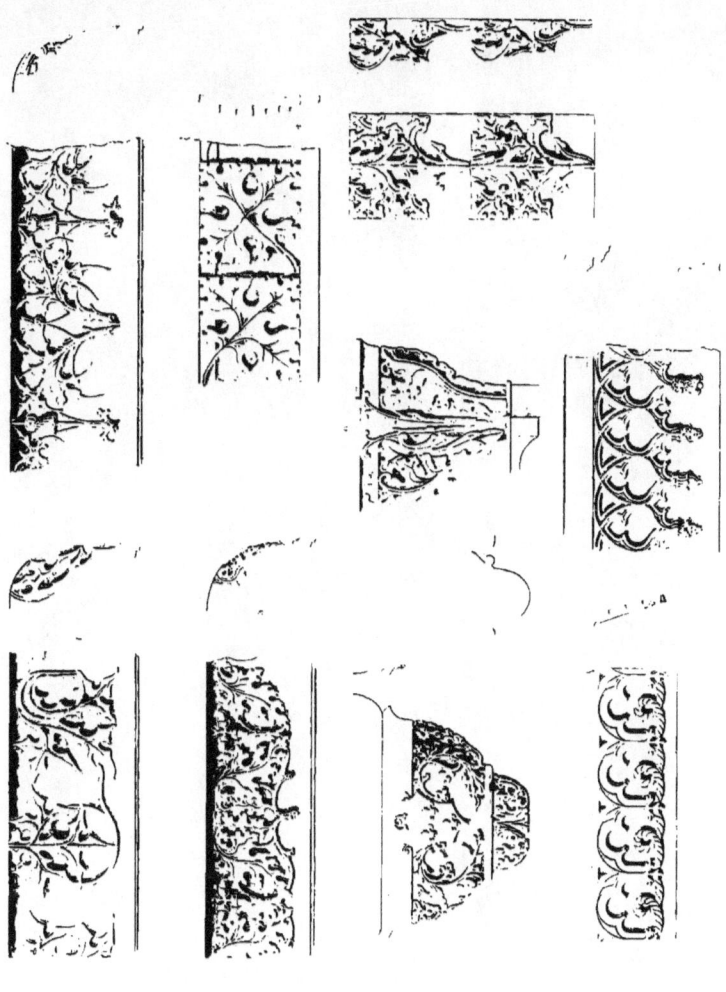

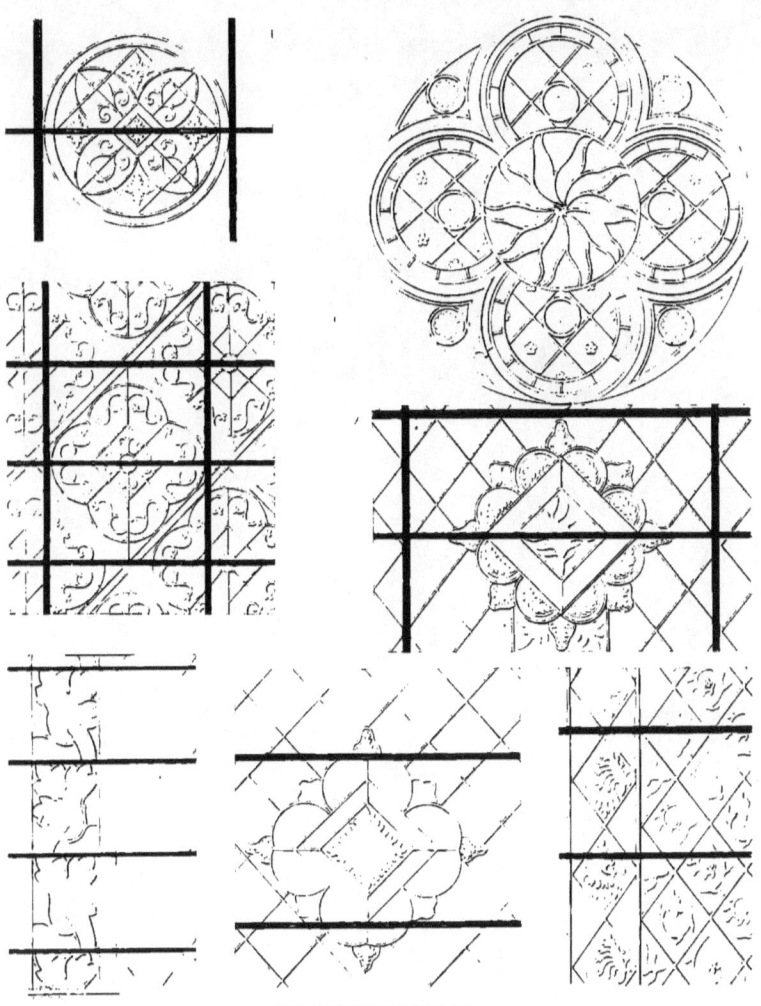

SEVEN SPECIMENS OF STAINED GLASS

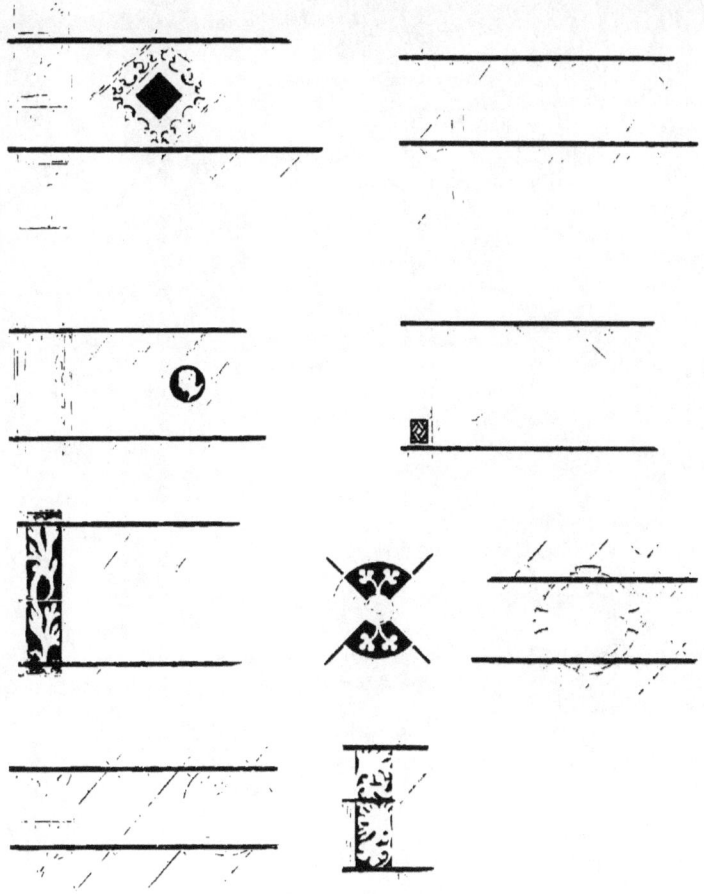

www.ingramcontent.com/pod-product-compliance
Lightning Source LLC
Chambersburg PA
CBHW021353230426
43666CB00006B/505